TRUMP THIS!

The Life and Times of Donald Trump:
An Unauthorized Biography

D1562446

NY Times Best-seller
MARC SHAPIRO

For more information contact:
Riverdale Avenue Books
5676 Riverdale Avenue
Riverdale, NY 10471.

www.riverdaleavebooks.com

Design by www.formatting4U.com
Cover by Scott Carpenter

Digital ISBN: 978-1-62601-263-9
Print: ISBN: 978-1-62601-264-6

First Edition February 2016

This Book is Dedicated to...

All the people who keep me honest and human with their love, understanding and encouragement. There isn't a whole lot to say that hasn't already been said a thousand times before.

My wife Nancy. My daughter Rachael. My granddaughter Lily. Brent, Robert and Layla. My agent Lori Perkins. Brady. Fitch (RIP).

All the real people who do the dirty jobs and truly deserve the credit. The creatives who often work their magic in the shadows. Good books. Good music. Good art.

And finally kudos to Donald Trump. He took the risk to put himself out there in a very big way. How many of us can say we've done the same?

TABLE OF CONTENTS

Author's Notes
How to Make a Trump

When approaching the life and times of Donald Trump, especially when you're a voter who might be thinking of nominating The Donald for the Republican candidate for President of the United States, (or an author trying to tell the tale) there is a lot to consider.

First there's the obvious. He knows business. Names like The Trump Tower, the Trump Plaza and Casino, and The Plaza Hotel roll off the tongue like butter. His string of successful hotels and golf courses are considerable and majestic. Even his time in the casino business and his days involved in less than successful ventures, such as Trump Wine and the Trump Board Game are stories well worth telling.

Then there's the idea of Trump the celebrity, *The Apprentice* host who, singlehandedly introduced the phrase 'you're fired!' into the daily nomenclature of our lives. The egotistical, arrogant comic book hero as flesh and blood upper class cock of the walk who is quick to insult, downgrade and basically verbally vaporize anybody strong enough or, for that matter, brave enough to cross swords and intimate that Donald Trump does not know everything about everything.

Because in his mind Donald Trump, physically and mentally, is sure that he does, indeed, know everything about everything.

Okay, that's pretty much Trump 101. The press and the political pundits have dissected and pontificated on The Donald with a fine-toothed comb for years. What they have come up with is no less worthy and significant, especially to those who have jumped on The Trump for President bandwagon in the last year. They want to know it all.

But does the public really want to know it all or are they just glomming onto what they're being fed and letting the rest go as insignificant or unnecessary to their often rabid following of The Donald? Those were some of the things I had to consider when looking for an angle for yet another Donald Trump tome.

Because there have been a lot of them. Some have been flattering to a fault (written by Trump himself or, more likely, with the aid of a smitten ghostwriter), others have been even-handed serious looks (courtesy of a seasoned journalist) and still others have been complete and blatant slams.

And of course there is that old devil 'bias' to throw into the mix. Since so many books on political figures (and just about anybody else with name recognition for that matter) have been written with a personal agenda, attitude or 'bias' in play, it's a legitimate question to ask if I have a beef with The Donald or am on the take in any way. The answer is no, no, a thousand times no. I have been thoroughly vetted by my publisher and deemed above board to write this book. But for those of you who don't believe anything or anybody (and yes I know you're out there), here's the abridged version of Marc Shapiro for Dummies.

I am a registered Democrat. I make no bones about it. But I have also been raised with an enquiring mind that is open to all possibilities. My parents were registered Democrats but they saw enough in Eisenhower to vote for him twice. I learned from my parents. When in doubt, go with your gut and the person you see as the best man for the job. I have not made a decision on Donald Trump yet. Where I'm at with this book is 'just the facts, ma'am' and let the chips fall where they may.

Which is ultimately the saner way to go with a subject who, in his personal and professional life, has been known to be slicker than Mercury and just as hard to handle.

Realistically, there have been many books and many attempts to dissect and figure out Donald Trump, many of which were written by Trump himself. In the hands of authors trying to make sense of this often Messianic creation, the emphasis seemed to be on the controversy, the alleged questionable and shady business dealings, and his failed marriages and relationships. You know, the kinds of things publishers feel, and rightly so, a book must contain at least a smidgen of to sell in this pop culture crazy, TMZ world. So ultimately what would make this book different?

The answer? How about keeping it simple?

We all have a good idea of what Donald Trump is. Let's give him the benefit of the doubt for a minute. Let's say he's some kind of a viable candidate, a bit unorthodox but still somebody who wants to do right by us. But he might more likely be a shill, a brand name in human form. Somebody with a bottom line for a soul and a bar code for a heart. Some think of him as some kind of God. Others think of him as a thing with horns and a long tail. But we're not casting aspersions here. What he is is ultimately up to you.

So how about a book chronicling the life that has molded, influenced and ultimately driven the larger-than-life character out into the world? There would be some easy, and not so easy, choices in his life. His parents for openers.

For better or worse we all had them and, let's be honest, a lot of who we are boils down to the attitudes of the people who raised us. Interaction with others... kids down the street and in school, teachers, girlfriends and wives. It's fun to speculate about what impact a young Candice Bergen turning down Trump's advances in college might have had on her suitor's already notorious ego. And just what drove a very young Trump to assault a teacher, which subsequently resulted in his parents shipping him off to military school, would seem an ideal talking point.

A different mindset was definitely involved in doing this book. A big consideration was that Trump, well below the surface, is a lot of things people would not expect from somebody with such a loudmouthed, bullying veneer. One could take nothing as truth or fiction without crosschecking until your eyes crossed. There was also the idea of being straight up, down the middle fair in telling his story. If somebody slammed Donald Trump, then the first thing I did was look for somebody who thought he was a Prince of a guy. And it went without saying that if Trump, in a manner of speaking, 'beat the rap' on a personal or professional matter, it was duly noted. Did I ever have a moment where I wanted to punch his face, call him a no good bullshit artist or, on the other hand, shake his hand? Sure did. But that's when a bit of psychology kicked in. Because Trump is not alone with his attitude and attributes. He's worked hard for his money, even though he has occasionally bent the rules a little bit and, in the name of fairness and, more importantly, good journalism, everybody deserves to know his yin and yang.

Get the picture? *Trump This! The Life and Times of Donald Trump* is about the moments in his life, good and bad, large and small, that combined to make Donald Trump something special in a whole lot of different worlds and, currently have made him a legitimate candidate for one of the biggest jobs on the planet...President of the United States.

About this time I can only imagine more than a few sets of eyeballs glazing over. Cue the cynics and the lazy whose response to going through Donald Trump's back pages is, "so what?"

Well I'll give you a so what?

There's a lot of risk and reward that goes into considering Donald Trump as President, even on a marginal/fantasy/science fiction level. President is a tough gig no matter how you slice it. I mean taking a pay cut to run a country isn't an easy thing to wrap your brain around. Trump in The White House would definitely be on-the-job training and more than a few people would have their fingers crossed.

In a best or worst-case scenario, a President

Trump could be the one to save our economy…or for that matter destroy it. How would you feel with President Trump as the final decision maker on whether we go to war or kick every non-US citizen out of the country? Presidents have to make nice to a lot of people, professionally and personally. Does Trump, who seems to live and die by the credo 'My way or the highway' have what it takes to get along? Remember this is the guy who could be guiding our fortunes and lives for the next eight years.

And Trump could, quite possibly, have his finger on the trigger of an intercontinental ballistic missile, sending who knows what to who knows where.

So yes, I think we do have a right to know just what makes a future leader tick.

Research, and a whole lot of it, has gone into the writing of this book. It is a book that has attempted to get into Donald Trump's head. To winnow out the things that have pushed him on to economic and celebrity status…

And that have left him primed and ready to take on the future.

Marc Shapiro 2016

Introduction
Nice Guys Finish Second

For the better part of summer and into fall 2015, Donald Trump was untouchable.

The business tycoon, multi billionaire, television celebrity and all around ego-driven high-flying real estate gadabout had gone from being the token freak show entry in the race for the Republican Presidential nominee to a constant frontrunner in every poll and to regularly best his more conservative and tradition-bound competitors by as much as 30 points.

Over the course of three months, Trump's stump speeches became an unexpected part of the pop culture landscape. Every time he'd open his mouth, The Donald (as he had long ago been dubbed by the media) was mouthing outrageous, controversial and, depending on how your politics roll, extremist and often borderline-racist views. Political and social organizations were taking numbers to see who could most loudly, figuratively take off his head and go for his throat. He had seemingly overnight become the defacto candidate that everybody loved to hate and most likely the one that a good many people agreed with and were willing to vote for.

From the outset, Trump was far from the stereotypical man of the people. He was almost laughingly unbelievable as the religious champion of blue-collar conservative values. Trump was more a carnival barker than a presidential candidate, his unorthodox approach often beginning and ending with him playing the 'class and money card' to audiences that, in almost all cases, were nowhere near his station in life.

When he first announced as a presidential candidate, Trump stated for the assembled press and, later in the pages of *Rolling Stone,* "I'm really rich." He would elaborate on his wealth in the very first Republican debate when he introduced himself by saying "I'm Donald Trump. I've made billions and billions of dollars making deals all over the world."

By contrast, his more traditional, sedate and conservative veteran politicians and fellow candidates were seemingly missing in action amid a wash of bland personalities and by the number talking points; occasionally offering weak attacks against Trump but ultimately putting up little in the way of a fight. Even the most impatient pundits, who loudly proclaimed that it would be only a matter of time before Trump's show would get old and he would soon fade to obscurity, had to acknowledge that Trump, at least to this point, had found the magic spell amid a growing populace that had it up to their eyeballs with old school politics.

But for those willing to look below the surface of Trump's egotistical, television reality show spin on what most perceived as an important moment in political history, it was a true life look at Trump and what made him tick.

Trump may not be a rocket scientist, although I'm sure he would tell you differently, but he does possess the very thing that has made him successful in the often ruthless worlds he lives in—business and now politics. To many, he's a clown. But the reality is that Trump is a master manipulator, a P.T. Barnum who can make anybody believe anything at the drop of a hat. If Trump were a professional gambler, one would be foolish to not bet with him. Because even if the cards said differently, Trump could easily convince the house that he had won.

In the fall of 2015, with the first state Presidential Republican primary nearly four months away, many were secretly conceding that the race was already over and that it would be Trump vs. Clinton in the final race to The White House.

Until late in October 2015, when something unexpected happened. Trump had suddenly fallen to second place in Iowa behind the other so-called 'outsider' in the race, retired neurosurgeon Ben Carson. It was a shock to observers and it suddenly gave hope to those struggling well down in the polls. As for Trump himself, who claimed in a CNN conversation that he had "been a counter puncher" on the campaign trail when it came to attacks by others, he had suddenly reverted to a relatively calm stance in explaining his reaction to suddenly being in second place.

"I don't really understand it [the poll numbers]," he told CNN. "We've been drawing great crowds and the people seem to be totally behind what I have to say. I guess I'll just have to work harder. Because I don't like being second in anything. I don't think anybody does."

Not only is 'second' an anathema for Trump, it is the concern and, perhaps subconsciously, what has driven him throughout his life; that and the cocksureness that he was born to be on top. In Trump's world, there never is a question of limits because Trump, in his own ego-driven, quite logical (at least to him) worldview, there are always new worlds to conquer and there is no reason why he shouldn't conquer them all.

It would easily take a full volume to dissect the many moods and personalities of Trump. But depending on whom you talk to, one comes away with the feeling that he is very much a creature of emotion and the moment.

In a detailed profile in *The New York Times*, there were many who stepped forward, often with tongue firmly planted in cheek, to describe Trump as a ragged and raw saint. Francis L. Bryant, a business associate from Manufacturer's Hannover Trust observed that, "Mr. Trump appears to be a wild man. He is not. Donald stays home. He sticks to what he knows." And no less a light than the Reverend Norman Vincent Peale (minister to many Republican presidents and bestselling author of The *Power of Positive Thinking*) extolled Trump's virtues when he described Trump as, "kindly and courteous in certain business negotiations and has a profound streak of honest humility."

But Trump can have a vindictive side as well. According to excerpts from a *Vanity Fair* article, part of a detailed look at Trump's character and temperament in Gronda Morin.com, *Spy Magazine* took a long and lingering shot in a 1988 article on Trump when it described the then budding tycoon "as a short fingered vulgarian. A bombastic, self-aggrandizing un-self-aware bully with a curious relationship with the truth."Trump immediately responded with threats of a lawsuit and followed up by sending the magazine a copy of his book *The Art of The Deal* with a note that promised, "If you hit me, I will hit you back 100 times harder."

That Trump's response to things not going his way seems like a walk through high school and playground politics and just plain bullying is part and parcel of his makeup. Like it or not, Trump's success in the adult world is very much balanced by an immature, juvenile streak. It was particularly evident in a book entitled *Never Enough: Donald Trump and the Pursuit of Success* in which two of his ex-wives cut to the chase.

Marla Maples described her former husband as "The little boy that still wants attention." Ivana Trump was equally succinct in describing Trump. "He wants to be noticed."

That the threat of a lawsuit came up early in his dealings with *Spy* is indicative of the fact that Trump and the threat of legal action are not strangers. In an article for *The Daily Beast*, writer Olivia Nuzzi chronicled a seemingly never-ending series of instances where he has sued, in no particular order, businesses, people, entire cities and countries, his ex-wife, a business card store and an entire Indian tribe for various 'alleged' offenses as breach of contract, government favoritism, fraud and libel. And in her piece, Nuzzi made a strong case for just why Trump sues at the drop of a hat.

"Trump sues when he is made to feel small, insufficiently wealthy, threatened or mocked. He sues for sport and he sues to regain control and he sues to make a point. He sues as a means of saying 'you're fired' to those he does not employ. But he sues, most of all, to make headlines and to reinforce the notion that he is powerful."

Trump's quirkiness has often been part and parcel of his larger than life persona and the controversy that, forever, seems to follow his every move. Such was the case in a revealing 1990 *Vanity Fair* profile in which it was disclosed by no lesser light than Trump's soon to be ex-wife Ivana that her husband kept a copy of the book *My New Order*, a book of Adolph Hitler's collected speeches, in a cabinet by his bed. Most likely, many would speculate, was that the book served as inspiration for the tycoon's daily battles in the business world.

When approached about this in the same *Vanity Fair* article, Trump seemed surprised and then attempted to rewrite the incident, stating that the book had, in fact, been *Mien Kampf* and that a Jewish friend had given it to him. When his statement would ultimately be contradicted, Trump assembled a weak response to confessing that he may, indeed, have possessed a copy of *My New Order*. "If I had those speeches, and I'm not saying that I do, I would never read them."

Nobody would ever be brave enough or, for that matter, stupid enough, to call Trump a liar, but there seemed to be a lot in his history of controversies and outrageous remarks that adheres to the real spontaneity of the man. He ultimately seems to be a man of the moment, saying what he says in a manner that rings just true enough and paints him in the best possible light.

It is a win at all costs attitude that has made Trump an alternately dynamic, obnoxious, driven character, known for shooting from the hip, not fearing to offend, as witnessed by his announcing his run for president in June 2015. In typical Trump manner, the billionaire descended an escalator in his famed business epicenter, Trump Tower, his hair, always a topic of conversation (is it real or is it Memorex?) blowing haphazardly in the slightest breeze, amid much pomp and circumstance. Once in front of the microphone, Trump made his announcement. It was raw, unrehearsed and from the first words, observers were alternately aghast and incensed at the stream of consciousness that came forth. If Trump had planned his presidential announcement, it sure did not seem that way. There was nothing somber and calm about it. At the moment he declared for the highest office in the land, Trump was very much a flailing carnival barker, intent on inciting the masses with style rather than substance.

In no particular order, Trump succeeded in slamming illegal immigrants as rapists, the way the economy was being run into the ground by a weak government and how he would bring other nations, both militarily and economically, to their knees. He called President Obama weak, said he would bring in a George S. Patton style General to bring the American military back to a once powerful state, all done to a backdrop of waving American flags and a whole lot of assurance directed straight at the common man, the blue collar working stiff who had, for a long time, felt he was getting the short end of the stick.

In fact, most of Trumps' support, from the beginning, has been from the heartland; an economic, educational and working class counter to Trump's upper-class, privileged and pampered résumé. But it is in this arena, as it would play out in whistle stop appearances to massive crowds and several candidate debates throughout the summer and into the fall, that Trump was the perfect political ringmaster; telling people exactly what irked them most and then promising his people that he would most certainly fix every problem. That he did not seem to have a nuts and bolts solution to any of these problems did not seem to bother anyone save the increasingly exasperated press corps who, during the seemingly endless interviews, would ask Trump for specifics and come away empty.

Ultimately Trump's campaign has boiled down to the simple equation of Trump being Trump and a large segment of the populace getting on board. And as the months rolled on, the inevitable gaffs, misspoken comments and revealing new discoveries about his past—things that bedevil most candidates—bounced off Trumps' well-manicured persona like so many bullets off Superman's chest, summarily dismissed by many as simply Trump being Trump.

Going into November and December 2015, Trump would occasionally pull back on the bombast and the outrageous, incendiary comments in favor of a more civilized and sedate approach to politicking. But those would only be temporary reprieves from the moment when he was attacked and that attack, in his opinion, required a verbal left hook. And there were many lining up to hear the latest bit of philosophy from Trump.

Unlike the rest of the Republican candidates, who were seemingly struggling to get crumbs of television and media attention, Trump had cultivated a persona in his first months on the stump to have the biggest news organizations blatantly currying favor and interviews amid the perception that Trump had emerged from a non-traditional political world to become the prohibitive favorite in state electoral primaries that were still months away. It seemed that every host on *CNN* was giving Trump face time, as were the big three national television networks, and off-beat appearances like the November hosting duties on *Saturday Night Live*.

For viewers, it was all a vicarious reality show. For Trump the fawning of the media was very much a world with which he was familiar. Trump meant ratings, money and ultimately the power of the super-rich and influential to bend people to his will.

Trump was certainly showing his true colors and personas. Many continued to dismiss him as playing a mind game on the country for whatever reason that made sense to him. With the Iowa caucus looming large in the coming year, the true impact of Trumps' prowess and potential would soon be tested.

In the meantime, it would just be more of Trump being Trump. And we all want to know to what degree his roots had in bringing him to this point.

Chapter One
The Family Tree

Experience may well be the best teacher, but a glance along the branches of Donald Trump's family tree indicates that his almost animal like pursuit of the bait of high rolling deal making, real estate expansion and the lofty heights of entrepreneurship and economic world building may well have had their roots in genes passed down through three generations of the Trump line.

Little has come to light about the Trumps before that time. What is known is that the Trump ancestral roots are German; specifically great-grandparents Christian Johannes Drumph (born 1829) and Katherina Kober (born 1836) who were born, lived their lives, married, had three children, and died all within the confines of Kallstadt, Pflaz, Germany.

That future generations of the Trump line were decidedly German, but Trump, two generations and many years later, would write in his book *The Art of The Deal*, that his family was Swedish in origin. Trump's own father, Fred Trump, would set the record straight in a *Vanity Fair* article when he revealed that he told people he was Swedish as a business move because, at the time, he was renting apartments in a building he owned to predominantly Jews who he feared would not rent from him if they knew he was German. Subsequently Trump would align himself with his father's version and would, over the years, embrace his German roots.

And as reported by *The New York Times, Politico.com, GenealogyAbout.com, The Daily Mail, The Seattle Times, Up Here Magazine* and many others, the beginning of the Trump way of doing business would begin with the true-life adventures of the Drumph's firstborn son.

Many in search of Trump's business acumen pointed to the birth of Christian and Katerina's first child, Frederich (born 1869) as the beginning of the Trump business model. Always a seemingly restless spirit, Friedrich bristled at the notion of following in the family footsteps, working the fields of their farm and supplementing the meager income as a barber. After the death of his father in 1877, young Friedrich began seeing his world as limited and, even at a young age, was manic in wanting to see what the rest of the world had to offer.

And so one night in 1885, after leaving a note to be discovered the next morning by his mother, the then16 year-old Friedrich snuck out into the night and made his way to Hamburg where he got on a ship called the Eider and made his way to America. Friedrich made good use of his early time in the US, eking out a meager living as a barber on the streets of New York, living in immigrant housing shelters and, perhaps most importantly, learning to speak English. He was also one who, instinctively, kept his eye on the events of the day. And when, in 1891, he heard along the grapevine that gold had been discovered in Seattle, Washington and literally hundreds of thousands of people were making their way west in a manic attempt to make their fortune, he followed the tide west. But it was not gold fever that was driving the young man.

Working more on gut instinct than any inside knowledge, Friedrich went to a notorious red light district called *The Lava Beds*, bought out an abandoned storefront he christened *The Poodle Dog* and converted it into a could-not-miss combination restaurant/bar and brothel. Friedrich had guessed right and, through the early 1890's, it proved to be a successful venture. Friedrich celebrated this success by doing the right business thing, Americanizing his name to Frederick Trump and becoming a naturalized citizen.

Throughout the 1890's, Frederick followed gold fever and its countless pursuers to places like Monte Cristo, Washington and Bennett, British Columbia, Canada, and the Klondike/Yukon vistas building continuously profitable restaurant/hotel/ brothel stop-overs for prospectors. Along the way, Frederick had become the consummate businessman, playing the angles and sometimes stretching the legality of land ownership laws, to end up by the end of the decade, a very wealthy man.

But by the end of the decade, the writing was on the wall. The gold rush had reached its peak and the whole concept of getting rich quick was fading, as was the impending crackdown on prostitution. Frederick knew it was time to sell off his 'establishments' and return to the life of a 'respected' businessman. And in Frederick's mind, being respectable meant getting married and starting a family.

Frederick returned to Kallstadt and eventually married his childhood neighbor Elisabeth Christ. Frederick would have been quite content to settle down and live happily ever after in the town he grew up in. But the German government would have none of it. They looked back in their records and discerned that Frederick had left the country, years earlier, to avoid Germany's tax and military obligations. Consequently, Frederick and his new bride were unceremoniously expelled from the country of their birth.

The couple returned to the US, specifically New York, where Frederick lived a much more sedate life as a barber and a restaurant manager. In his later years, he would dabble in real estate development, not being able to completely give up the business practices that had allowed him to amass his fortune. In 1905, the couple's first child, Fred Trump Jr. was born.

From the very beginning, Fred Trump proved to be a compelling example of the apple not falling far from the tree. He was a bright, inquisitive boy who absorbed information like a sponge; in particular the late-in-life real estate workings of his father. He also spent a lot of time looking over the shoulder of his mother, Elisabeth, who handled the books and wrote the checks for the couple's company, subsequently immersing himself in all aspects of the business.

Friederick was quick to notice his boy's interest and happily brought his barely pre-teen son into the real estate and development world. So quickly, in fact, that the *Hely Times* reported that Fred Jr. by the age of 15, had made enough money in the business to pay his younger brother's way through college. Fred Trump had found his niche in life. Ironically Trump's father,

Frederick, would not live to see his son's earliest forays into the family business as he died in 1918 after coming down with pneumonia during a nationwide flu epidemic.

The family moved, as chronicled in *Hubpages.com*, instinctively into survival mode. Elisabeth began working as a seamstress while Fred took whatever odd jobs he could find, which entailed everything from delivery boy to shoe shine boy, and hauling lumber at construction sites. The notion of being around construction sites and watching, firsthand, as America was literally created, building by building, fascinated Fred and so he set about learning the ins and outs of the building trade, taking classes in carpentry, plan reading and estimating.

Fred celebrated his newfound passion when, at the ripe old age of 16, he built his first structure, a two-car frame garage for a neighbor. Inspired by this first building, he began his own business, building prefabricated garages for $50 each. Fred continued to hone his skills, working as a carpenter's helper for a home-builder in Queens.

There was sadness and, given their German heritage, much stoicism in the Trump house with Frederick's passing. But it almost went without saying that Fred would jump full time into the family business. By the late 1920's, the by then 22-year old Trump had built and sold his first home and had decided to go full on into the real estate development and construction business, forming with Elizabeth, his equally business-minded mother, *Elisabeth Trump & Son Co*.

It was also in the late 20's that Fred had his first brush with infamy. A quiet man who was not prone to airing his political and social views in public, Fred, in a June 1927 issue of *The New York Times*, was suddenly tarred with a racist brush when a story revealed, almost after the fact, that Fred and six others, reportedly members of the Ku Klux Klan, had been arrested in a May skirmish between 1000 KKK members and 100 police officers in Queens, New York in which several officers were, reportedly, beaten. The article named Fred by his full name and his address. According to the article, Fred, along with the other alleged Klan members, was arrested and arraigned. That Fred was not only a member of the KKK and had been involved in the brawl was wildly hinted at but, ultimately, enough grey areas appeared to put the question of Trump's involvement in doubt and it quickly passed from the public's mind; only to resurface in 2015 when several websites rediscovered the article and speculated that like father like son, alleged racist attitudes seemed to run in the Trump family.

The elder Trump had been too busy with his life to consider any lingering consequences of the article and allegations. At the time, the 21-year-old Trump was too busy getting his professional life off the ground.

His first successful foray into big business was the construction of single family homes in the Queens area of New York City. Fred would prove an instinctive pioneer in the coming real estate boom when, at the height of The Great Depression in the 30's, he built the *Trump Market*, a very early supermarket concept and, not surprisingly, sold it a year after it opened to a larger supermarket chain for a massive profit.

It was right in the middle of Fred's professional rise (1936) that he met and married a recent Scottish immigrant, Mary Anne MacLeod. Their immediate attraction and marriage was quick and in the tenor of the times. Within a year, the couple would have the first of what would ultimately be five children.

By 1939, when World War II was officially declared, Fred was continuing to capitalize on America's involvement; building barracks and apartments for the navy and, ever the futurist, seeing a not too distant future in which hundreds of thousands of veterans would be returning to the states and in need of low budget housing which he was already making plans to build.

Shortly after World War II came to a close in 1945, Mary Anne MacLeoud went into labor for the fourth time. Donald John Trump would come kicking, screaming and, reportedly very demanding, into the world on June 14, 1946. It would be considered mere coincidence that the United States of America on that same day would declare *Flag Day* an official holiday.

Chapter Two
My Way

By the time Donald Trump was born, his father Fred had evolved into a bit of a homebody. His sphere of influence as a real estate developer and builder had been concentrated primarily in the boroughs of Queens, Brooklyn and Staten Island. Rarely did his work take him any further and he was seemingly quite content with his life and work now concentrated in this relatively small outpost. Consequently, with his family expanding and his business life now settled into a fairly comfortable routine, Frederick did not have to look far to find a place to put down roots... in the hilly and wealthy area of *Jamaica Estates*.

Founded in the borough of Queens in 1907, Jamaica Estates—nestled in a pocket surrounded by the Union Turnpike, Hillside Avenue, Utopia Parkway and 188th Street—had, by the 1940's, gradually evolved into a family friendly sanctuary for those upper middle class working families who worked, primarily in New York City proper but who craved a quiet sanctuary away from the hustle and bustle of big city life.

Years later, in a *New York Times* article, Trump would matter-of-factly dissect the notion that Jamaica

Estates was literally an oasis surrounded by the real world. "Different parts of Queens were rough; this [Jamaica Estates] was an oasis. Jamaica Estates was safe."

Fred had grown up in and around Jamaica Estates and, not surprisingly, he would not venture out from his familiar surroundings when it came to laying down permanent roots for his ever-expanding family.

"My father lived there in the same house on Midland Parkway up until his death," Trump recalled in conversation with *The Real Deal.com*. "My father loved Queens and he loved Brooklyn and that's where he did his business. He never came to Manhattan."

Trump, in later years, would acknowledge that his father was insular in his life, steadfastly refusing the lucrative prospects of branching out, professionally, into a wider world. But, in a conversation with *Playboy,* he conceded that there was no arguing that his father was truly successful, albeit in a limited way.

"My father never really got away from Brooklyn and Queens," he recalled. "He was very successful there. You have to be comfortable with what you're doing or you won't be successful."

At a very early age, Trump had evolved into a bright, inquisitive and, by infant small steps, his own person. Thanks in no small part from the quite different influences handed down from his parents. Trump would recall in a conversation with *The Real Deal.com* that, even as an infant, he could sense a loving interaction between his father and himself, centered to a large extent, on his father's drive and passion for his work. "I learned so much from my father. He enjoyed what he did so much. I saw that and it kind of rubbed off on me."

To the extent that, by age five, Trump would willingly go along with his father and observe intently when he would go to inspect building and construction sites. His relationship with his father, cemented by the elder Trump's work, would escalate with the years and, by the age of 13, would result in Trump often being seen driving a bulldozer around a work site.

But in a very different and ultimately equally important way, Trump derived much of the influences that would guide him as an adult from his mother. On the surface, Mary Anne MacLoud had appeared the almost stereotypical Scottish immigrant housewife and mother. In a conversation with radio talk show host Hugh Hewitt, Trump was quick to describe his mother "as being very religious." But in a *Business Insider* excerpt from Trump's book *The Art of The Deal,* Trump offered that there was more to his mother's influence than his early Presbyterian upbringing.

"Looking back, I realize now that I got some of my sense of showmanship from my mother. She always had a flair for the dramatic and the grand. She was a very traditional housewife but she also had a sense of the world beyond her."

Trump's relationship with his siblings was set from an early age, as he became more influential in the family business. As the years went by, his younger brother Robert, who would eventually work for him and his sisters Maryanne and Elizabeth, would, allegedly, be the followers rather than the leaders and would agree with just about everything Trump put on the familial table.

Although the consensus has always been that, with the exception of older brother Fred, the Trump siblings had always gotten along in a cordial manner, one would be hard pressed to find anything but generalities about how the Trump children interacted. With the exception of older sister Maryanne, a judicial star herself, Trump rarely said a word about his brothers and sisters.

However, in his victory speech at the New Hampshire primary, Trump took a rare moment to acknowledge Maryanne, who would go on to have quite the career in the judicial world as a Federal Circuit Court Judge of the United States Court of Appeals for the Third Circuit and the recipient of a Sandra Day O'Connor Award. And when asked by *The Washington Post*, Trump was quick to take notice of her achievements. "She loves what she's doing. She's highly respected. She's considered one of the truly brilliant people in the Federal Court. She's a big federal judge at a very high level." However, he added, that should he be elected president, he would not appoint her to the Supreme Court.

Looking back, Trump would seem thoroughly satisfied with those early years in a 2005 conversation with *CNN*. "I really grew up pretty normal. I lived in an upper middle-income area. It was nice. It was just good."

The Trump family seemed to fit easily into the fabric of Jamaica Estates from the moment they moved into the 23-room mansion on Midland. And to their neighbors, the Trump family seemed to be a contradiction of attitudes, according to a *New York Times* article that, years later, would venture back into Trump's Jamaica Estates neighborhood.

Fred Quint, a former Trump neighbor, related to

The New York Times that he would see the elder Trump leave for work every day in a chauffeured blue Cadillac limousine. At the other end of the scale, several of those interviewed in the article stated that the Trumps did their own shopping and that they would often see the parents at the local supermarket, bagging their own groceries.

What is known about Trump's childhood seems to center around the fact that he was brought up in a strict and no-nonsense home where hugs and kisses from his parents were rare according to those who lived near the family. And the result seems to have been that Trump, by the age of five, had turned into what neighbors considered hyper-competitive, controlling and a bit of a neighborhood bully.

Laura Manuelidis, who lived behind the Trump house as a child, related to *The New York Times* how when playing ball, she would often encounter the wrath of Trump. She recalled that if a ball she was playing with happened to go into the Trump's yard, she would be greeted by an irate young Trump who, not only would not toss the ball back, but would threaten to tell his dad and to call the police.

And Trump's acting out was not confined to the neighbors. His younger brother, Robert, would often be on the losing end of verbal and physical tussles with his older brother. Such as the time his brother browbeat him into giving up his blocks for a project Trump was working on and never got them back.

The young Trump soon became a literal menace to the neighborhood. Parents had taken an immediate dislike to him and, in several instances, had forbidden their children from associating with him. To Trump's parents, where perception and image had always been in the forefront of society and business, their son's acting out must have caused an anxious moment but, if it had, Fred was quick to underplay his son's childhood bullying and intimidation.

"He [Donald] was a pretty rough fellow when he was small," Fred disclosed to *The New York Times.*

Trump's parents were seemingly well aware of their young son's aggressive and assertive nature but apparently did little if anything to curtail it; preferring to chalk it up to normal childhood acting out.

Years later Trump would address his childhood antics in his book *The Art of The Deal*, as reported by *Business Insider*, when he quipped, "I liked to stir things up and I liked to test people."

But as Trump turned old enough to enter formal education, it has been speculated that his rambunctiousness might make him a target for ostracism or worse in the public school setting. Not surprisingly, Fred's business acumen has succeeded in the family currying a lot of political and social favor and influence in many areas of Queens and Jamaica Estates business and social life.

Along the way, Fred had become a board member and a major donor to the prestigious *Kew-Forest School* in Queens. And if that was not enough grease, Jerome Tuccille's book, *The Saga of America's Most Powerful Real Estate Baron*, chronicles how Fred would often 'loan' the institution free building materials and, in one instance, free use of one of his construction crews for an expansion project at the school. Consequently, as Tuccille stated in his book, "The question of disciplining Donald was one that had to be handled delicately as Fred Trump was too valuable an asset to risk alienating him."

Which, upon entry to *Kew-Forest School* would appear to give Trump carte blanche to act out and create havoc. During his years at the school, Trump's acting out and hijinks, according to Tuccille's book, consisted of, among other things, squirting soda at girls and throwing erasers at teachers. That Trump could be prone to violence was made evident when, in the second grade, a then seven year-old Trump got into a disagreement with his music teacher, one that turned progressively more heated until finally fists started to fly.

"In the second grade I actually gave my teacher a black eye," Trump related in his book *The Art of The Deal*, as excerpted by *Business Insider*. "I punched my music teacher because I didn't think he knew anything about music. I'm not proud of that but it's clear evidence, even early on, that I had a tendency to stand up and make my opinions known in a very forceful way."

Hitting a teacher was automatic grounds for expulsion but, most likely with the influence of Trump's father, Trump got off fairly lightly with a period of detention, a punishment Trump would become quite familiar with during his years at Kew-Forest. So much so that Trump's friend at Kew-Forest, Paul Onish, told *National Public Radio*. "We used to refer to our detention as a DT, a Donny Trump, because he got more of them than most other people in the class."Onish related that Trump would also get into trouble for seemingly predictable school infractions; talking in class, passing notes and throwing spitballs.

How good a student Trump was during his years at Kew-Forest remains largely a mystery, with only a handful of reports, most notably *Trump's Education: Presidential Candidates.com* that would only go so far as to report that as a student at Kew-Forest, "Trump was not very good." But apparently, when he was not causing trouble, Trump was a very good athlete, playing football, soccer and showcasing a fairly lively fastball at grade school baseball level.

But at the end of the day, any good works he generated at Kew-Forest were ultimately undone by his constant battles with authority, his arrogance and a growing feeling from those who interacted with him that Trump basically suffered the classic rich kids sense of entitlement and feeling that because his family had money, nobody could tell him what to do. Consequently, Trump, by the time he completed the seventh grade at age 13, had become a regular topic of conversation in Jamaica Estates and most of what was being talked about was not good.

Trump's parents were not deaf to what was being said about their son and were growing more concerned as the reports of bad behavior from the school became more frequent. Trump's parents knew that their influence at the school and in the community would only engender so much good will and that reputation and perception could ultimately combine to sidetrack their son's life even before it started. And nobody was more aware of his status as a troublemaker than Trump, who conceded in an interview with *Playboy* that, essentially, he had been guilty as charged.

"I was very bad," he said. "I was not violent or anything but I wasn't exactly well behaved. I talked back to my parents and people in general. Perhaps it was more like bratty behavior. I certainly was not the perfect child."

But as he grew older, Trump's father, sensing that a dose of workingman's reality might do his children well, gave Trump and his brothers on the job training in the hardscrabble, blue collar world. As Trump would recall in a conversation with *Rolling Stone*, summers would find the Trump boys pulling weeds and pouring cement on work sites. "We went with our father to collect rents. We'd go on jobs where we needed tough guys to knock on doors. You'd see them ring a doorbell and then stand way over there. I'd say why were you over there? He [the tough guy] would say because those motherfuckers shoot right through the door."

Trump's life at Kew-Forest would finally come to an end shortly before he was due to enter the eighth grade. As documented in the book, *The Trumps: Three Generations That Built an Empire*, Trump and a close friend took it upon themselves to make an unauthorized trip into New York City to see a production of *West Side Story* on Broadway. The young boys were so enamored of the musical that they immediately went out and bought switchblades to get the vicarious charge of what they had seen on stage.

It was never reported that Trump and his friend had actually brought the knives onto the school campus. But when Trump's father found out, he reportedly hit the proverbial ceiling, telling his son his ongoing bad behavior must stop. Trump's parents were at their wits' end and, shortly thereafter, told their son that he would not being continuing his education at Kew-Forest.

Even at age 13, Trump had seemingly already developed a sense of reality unto himself and the world around him. Most 13 year olds would have likely thrown a fit at the idea of being summarily sent away. But Trump, looking back on the situation years later in conversation with *CNN,* just took it in stride. "I wasn't the most well behaved person in the world and my parents had no idea what to do with me. Then they heard of this school that was a real tough place."

Chapter Three
Military Minded

New York Military Academy was cut from traditional cloth. Located in upstate New York, NYMA had a long held reputation of taking young boys and turning them into young men with a steady diet of military style influences and physical and mental toughness that made them prime candidates for careers in the military, business and, yes, occasionally the arts. Their list of famous alumni ran the gamut from composer Stephen Sondheim and bandleader Les Brown to mobster John Gotti, Jr.

It was into this environment that Trump seemingly went willingly in 1959, even though early on he had been brought up in a pampered, millionaire home, and that might put him at a distinct disadvantage when he first entered New York Military Academy.

Ted Dobias, a retired World War II Colonel who at the time was a full time instructor at New York Military Academy, recalled in a *National Public Radio* interview that his first impression of Trump on that first day at the school was not encouraging. "I put him down at the end of the dormitory hall. He didn't know how to make a bed. He didn't know how to shine his shoes. He had a problem with being a cadet. He didn't know how to take care of himself."

But Dobias had seen the Trump kind before and he made it clear, in the *NPR* interview, to the new cadet that he was not going to cut him any slack. "I made it clear to him that I didn't care who his daddy was. When he got out of line he would get the same treatment as everybody else. Nobody was different. We treated everyone alike."

But Dobias would concede in a *Rolling Stone* interview that force feeding Trump a steady diet of the military life was not easy. "He [Trump] thought that he was Mr. America and that the world revolved around him. I had a lot of one-on-ones with him, some of which got physical."

Word about Trump's background and his inability to tie or shine his own shoes quickly spread among his fellow cadets. In his first days, he appeared headed for an early washout from the strict school and a prime candidate to be ostracized and picked on. But as author Gwenda Blair would note in her book *The Trumps: Three Generations of Builders and a Presidential Candidate*, Trump had a surprising reaction to being thrust into the military life. "Donald seemed to welcome being in a place with clear cut parameters, a place where he could focus on figuring out how to come out on top and get what he wanted."

To say that the young Trump adjusted quickly to his new environment was an understatement. Not only did he learn how to tie his shoes but he also was able to ease, comfortably, into a military way of order that saw him learning to say 'Yes sir! No sir!' and to salute, how to march and how to handle a gun. What

emerged early in his stay at New York Military
Academy was Cadet Trump, equal parts conformist
and competitor, with his long held arrogance and ego
tossed in for good measure. Within a traditionally rigid
military world, Trump was taking his first steps in the
direction of rugged individual. And his classmates
were quick to catch on.

Trump's former NYMA classmate, George
Beuttell, was particularly enamored of Trump's sense
of style and the way he presented himself, as he
explained in *Business Insider*. "He was a good man.
Nobody ever spoke badly about him back then and he
was well liked." Beuttell also acknowledged in the
same interview that while a lot of the kids at New
York Military Academy were not taking any of the
curriculum very seriously, Trump, once he set his
mind to it, definitely was. "He [Trump] had direction
back then that a lot of us other kids didn't. A lot of us
were fooling around, playing around and he was more
business than a lot of us."

By the end of his first year at NYMA, Trump had
definitely bought in to the military way of doing
things. Mike Kabealo, one of Trump's roommates
during his years at NYMA, indicated in a conversation
with *National Public Radio* that Trump was
determined to adhere to the military way of doing
things while developing a strongly competitive streak
and no small amount of arrogance. "He was cocksure,
positive and anything you can do I can do better kind
of stuff. He was very competitive."

Examples of Trump's competitive nature and
drive showed up at every turn. When he was put in
charge of the dorm's rifle rack, he was, according to

31

classmates, beyond obsessive about keeping the rifles clean. He saw his military school uniform as an extension of his own drive for perfection and kept it spotless. And when it was his turn to do room inspections, there would be hell to pay if his classmates' efforts were not up to Trump's standards. One person who recalled feeling the wrath of Trump was classmate Ted Levine who related in *National Public Radio* that failing a Trump inspection had once resulted in violence.

Levine stated that he had made his bed particularly tight but not to Trump's standards and Trump ripped the sheets off the bed. For Levine, that turned out to be the last straw. "I totally lost it. I hit him with a broomstick. Then he came back at me with his hands. He was bigger than me and it would take three people to get him off me."

Levine would room with Trump for a time and while he hinted that there were a couple of stories about life with Trump, he was reluctant to repeat them. However, he would concede that there had been a couple of fights between them, but explained that fighting was common at the school.

During his years at the academy, Trump had physically matured into a strapping 6'2" frame. His physical stature coupled with a seemingly natural athletic ability made him a three-sport standout in baseball (1962-64), football (1962) and soccer (1963). It was in the former sport that Ted Levine, whose relationship with Trump had slowly but surely evolved into a tolerant truce, told *Business Insider* that he was once again on the receiving end of Trump's power.

"I think he threw 80 miles an hour [as a pitcher],"

he related. "I was the catcher and he made my hand black and blue every day. He was just the best, a good athlete, a great athlete. He could have probably played pro ball as a pitcher.[In fact reports had surfaced indicating at least a couple of major league teams, including the Philadelphia Phillies, had been scouting Trump during his military academy years.] He could do anything he wanted. He was physically and mentally gifted."

Well, at least physically. The question has always remained how good a student Trump was in academic studies. The consensus has always been that Trump hit the books out of necessity while at NYMA. While he may not have been head of the class academically, he was doing more than enough to maintain his status as very good military academy material who was considered good enough to be named a Cadet Captain, a high honor at the academy, during his stay at NYMA.

The notion has been floated over the years that the young Trump's attitude may not have been conducive to making friends during his stay at NYMA. That was not necessarily the case. Reports from fellow classmates seem to indicate a more casual relationship rather than strong bonding in a way that has been a historical tradition in military schools. But that was not the case with Trump. A story examining Trump's academy years in *National Public Radio*, said the young cadet walked the campus with an obvious air of superiority, was quick to interrupt a fellow cadet in conversation with what has been described as a condescending laugh. It was apparent that Trump thought he was much better than the people around him.

And that, according to former classmate Levine in the *National Public Radio* story, made it difficult to get close to Trump. "I don't think he had a handful of loyalists. Because he was so competitive that everybody who would come close to him, he had to destroy."

But there would ultimately be grudging respect for Trump, as was offered in *Business Insider*. He fit in to the point where he was bestowed the nickname of 'D.T.' He also went by Don or Trump according to his classmates. And when it came to women, Trump soon gained the reputation as a Ladies' Man. Since New York Military Academy was an all-boys institution, it was rare that women were allowed on campus, usually only on Sundays.

However, come Sunday, Trump would often be seen in the company of beautiful and very uptown-looking women strolling the NYMA campus, often arm-in-arm. Classmate George White was among the cadets who would regularly marvel at Trump's ability to attract the ladies. "The type of women who were coming up to see him or he was bringing to the campus were definitely from the upper levels of New York society," White told *National Public Radio*. "I remember there were so many, it was like a revolving door."

Classmate Beuttell, likewise, told *Business Insider*, that Trump seemed like a prize to the women Trump was with during his military academy days. "He was a very good looking, handsome guy and he held himself in a way that everyone thought he'd be very desirable for the opposite sex."

But if and when Trump lost his virginity during

his military academy years is still open to conjecture and speculation. While in later years he would talk fairly freely about having sex with many women, he has remained conspicuously quiet about any conquests while at NYMA. The only clue to Trump's relationships with women in his formative years came in a conversation with *Business Insider* when he stated, "I always treated women with the greatest respect. I admire them."

By 1964, Trump had successfully managed to become a big fish in a relatively small pond. His diligence militarily had resulted in his being promoted to one of the highest ranks in the academy, Cadet Captain S4 (Battalion Logistics Officer) and, according to *Truthdig.com*, was managing a serviceable B average in the classroom. Trump had long since become restless with it all and constantly had his mind on the next big adventure in what he considered the real world.

Trump's future goals as he made his way through NYMA were not set in stone but they seemed fairly well laid out as far as specifics went. He wanted to make money, lots of money, and his inclination was to somehow follow in his father's real estate footsteps. But there had been long standing differences. The younger Trump seemed to gravitate towards the glitz and glamour of any situation rather than his father's tradition-bound, conservative approach to life. Consequently, when it came to what he was going to do with his life, he inevitably looked toward a future in the big city. In the sense that Trump seemed to crave drama and bigger than life adventures, he was very much like his mother.

Fred Trump's visions had stopped at the boroughs of Queens and Brooklyn. When, as a young boy, he would contemplate his life, Donald Trump looked further down the road—to the bright lights and big city of New York.

The New York Military Academy was steeped in tradition and one of its long-standing missions was its annual cadet march down Fifth Avenue during the city's Columbus Day Parade. It was during one such march, a march that would, coincidentally, take Trump past the building that would, years later, house The Trump Towers, that Trump made his intentions to become a real estate mogul public for the first time.

Classmate Jack Seraphin related the story, as it was told to him by Colonel Ace Castellano, in *Business Insider*. "At one point in the march, Donald turned to Ace and said, 'Ace, I'd like to get some of this real estate someday.' Ace looked at him and thought 'Boy he's full of himself...'

... But he's got some goals."

Chapter Four
Contrary to Popular Opinion

Trump graduated from the New York Military Academy in 1964. At that point the barely 18-year old was suddenly adrift with no concrete goals. One thing was certain. He wanted to make lots of money.

Having turned 18, Trump found himself obligated to register for the draft, which he did willingly according to a report in *The Washington Post* that chronicled the ins-and-outs of Trump's draft status. *The Washington Post* further quoted Trump as saying he would fight for his country if called. However, right after registering, he also filed for, and was granted, the first of what would be four education deferments. Now all he had to do was pick out a college to justify the deferment.

Initially his youthful mind went in the direction of the entertainment industry, thinking, as a lark, that he might attend the University of Southern California film school and become an actor, or before thinking much harder about making a living as a film producer or studio executive. But, as he recalled in his book *The Art of The Deal,* and was chronicled in an *Adweek* profile, he eventually changed his mind when he decided the real estate business would be more lucrative.

The consensus in Trump's inner circle was that the young man would now go back to working with his father and, eventually wind up taking over the family business. But even at that age, Trump was quite forward thinking and decided to further his education, matriculating at Fordham University and immersing himself in economics. As it turned out, Fordham University was not a big step; it was located in the nearby borough of The Bronx. While Trump's decision, given his long range worldview, may have seemed somewhat at odds, Trump saw nothing but logic in his decision as was reported in an article on his college years published by *The Globe*.

Quite simply, Trump was homesick.

"I had very good marks and I was a good student, generally speaking. But I wanted to be home for a couple of years. I was away for five years. So I wanted to spend time home and to get to know my family again."

Despite all the self-proclaimed greatness he was achieving during his two years at Fordham, the reality was that Trump's years at that university were nondescript in the extreme. What fragments of Trump's years at Fordham have come to light indicate that he was doing just enough to get by and not really exerting himself, did not really embrace college life and was essentially coasting through his two years at the university. The result of all this, according to the book *Donald Trump: Master Apprentice* by Gwenda Blair, was that Trump's grades at Fordham were no better than "respectable."

In his book *The Art of The Deal*, Trump gave a backhanded acknowledgement of Fordham and the student body while acknowledging his restlessness. "I began by attending Fordham University but, after two years, I decided that, as long as I had to be in college, I might as well test myself against the best."

In the book *Donald Trump: Master Apprentice*, Trump acknowledged that Fordham's emphasis on Economics was not really his thing and that he was more interested in business development, "the what if kind of stuff."

The Wharton School of Business at The University of Pennsylvania seemed to fit the bill. Established as the very first business school in the United States in 1881, The Wharton School of Business had status written all over it. The very private Ivy League university was expensive, prestigious and upheld a stringent entry process that made it next to impossible for even the most business savvy and intellectually inclined student to get in. And Trump's chances, squeaking by with respectable grades at Fordham and attempting a transfer to an undergraduate program in his third year, did not bode well in a school that typically had 8,000 applicants applying for 1,700 slots.

But Trump was, if nothing else, beholden to his family to the extent that, while not looking forward to another two years in any university, he agreed to go to Wharton for his father's sake, according to Jerry Tuccillein his biography *Trump: The Saga of America's Most Powerful Real Estate Baron*. And, as it turned out, Trump was not above using his family's influence to grease the wheels at Wharton.

In her book *The Trumps: Three Generations of Builders That Built an Empire,* author Gwenda Blair stated that Trump gained admission as a transfer student from Fordham because of an interview with a Wharton admissions officer who was a former classmate of Trump's older brother Freddy. Blair also speculated that being the son of one of New York's wealthiest businessmen might well have played a part in Trump gaining entry to Wharton.

Not surprisingly, Trump painted a different picture in a conversation with *The Boston Globe*. "I got in quickly and easily to the Wharton. And it's one of the hardest schools to get into in the country."

Trump arrived on the Wharton campus in 1966 behind the wheel of a flashy Ford Fairlane. And the car he was driving was only a preview of the bombast and braggadocio that marked his entry into the school's undergraduate program. During his first day in class Trump gave notice to teachers and fellow classmates that, at least in his own mind, he was the real deal.

Louis Colomaris was a classmate of Trump's during that first year and recalled in a conversation with *The Boston Globe* the first day in a real estate class in which the professor's innocent question opened the Trump floodgates. "When the professor asked his students why they had chosen to study real estate, Trump said, 'I'm going to be the King of New York Real Estate.' I was sitting there thinking, 'Sit down you [expletive].' That was our introduction to Donald Trump."

But that fiery introduction would quickly be replaced, much as it had been in his years at Fordham, by a Trump who seemingly faded into the woodwork and, finally, obscurity. While those who knew him claimed that he would regularly speak up and contribute to class discussions, there was never anything overly brilliant about what he had to say. He reportedly avoided campus life at all costs, shunning social activities, frat parties and presented a focused and aloof image on campus, a business-like style of sports coats and jackets that ran contrary to the preppy couture of tweed coats and polka dot ties much in evidence at Wharton.

At a time when political and social revolution was in the air on college and university campuses, Trump steered clear, especially when it came to the growing anti-Vietnam War protests and unrest on campus. "I wasn't a fan of the Vietnam War," Trump told *The Boston Globe*. "But I wasn't a marcher."

Living in off-campus, roach-infested apartments throughout his stay at Wharton would seem to have softened his superiority complex, but not by much. His veneer of being better than everybody else and his totally self-centered attitude were never far from the face he showed his classmates. Trump did develop a couple of culinary quirks while at Wharton. He became obsessed with the fried oysters that were on the menu at a nearby Howard Johnsons' and was a regular at the bar called the *Bull and Barrel* on the nights it offered up 20-cent hamburger specials.

But at the end of the day, Trump at Wharton barely registered in the student body consciousness. At least when *The Daily News* came calling. Classmate Nancy Hano said, "Trump was not known on campus for any reason at all." Another former classmate, Stanton Koppel, said, "I have no memory of him at all."

And that may well have been because, when not in class, Trump was already conducting business.

Upon arrival at Wharton, Trump had been quick to size up the local housing market and, in particular, the number of run-down, less than desirable buildings in the Pennsylvania area. He saw potential, much in the way his father always had, and went to Frederick with the idea of making his first official foray into the real estate business by buying up neglected properties, fixing them up and selling them for a profit. All he needed was up start-up capital, which was where his father came in.

Trump's father was impressed at his son's proposal as well as his initiative. After listening patiently, Frederick, according to a piece in *The Boston Globe*, agreed to loan his son $2 million to get his enterprise off the ground. Trump did not waste any time busting his cherry on his first solo real estate venture, one that marked his instinct on how to play the real estate game. "I didn't want people to know I was buying because once they started knowing your name, the price goes up. So I would use aliases, corporate names or different names."

The result was that, while Trump admitted to making only a little bit of money while at Wharton, he would eventually pay back his father's loan, a strong professional and emotional point with Trump, and arrive as a full blown player in the real estate game. "It's always been a natural instinct," Trump told *The Boston Globe* of that early success. "I would buy little houses and buildings, fix them up, sell them, rent them and do all sorts of things."

Trump's ambition was in direct contradiction to that of his older brother Freddy who had forsaken the family business in favor of becoming a pilot. Freddy also liked to drink a lot and was well on the way to being a full-blown alcoholic, complications of which would lead to his premature death at age 43. Needless to say, being polar opposites often made for combustible moments when the Trump boys got together.

In a recent piece that focused on the older Trump, *The New York Times* painted a picture of the second son who was impatient with what he viewed as the non-traditional antics of Freddy. Social get-togethers could be particularly tense according to a member of Freddy's social circle, Annamaria Schilano. "I was at a dinner with Freddy and Donald got real upset with Freddy and told him to grow up, get serious and to make something of himself in the family business. Donald put Freddy down quite a bit. He would pick fights with Freddy and then storm out. There was a lot of combustion."

In the same article, a candid Trump would concede that he learned a lot from what he perceived as his older brother's self-destructive ways. "I learned by watching my brother how bad choices could drag down even those who seemed destined to rise. Seeing my brother suffer led me to avoid alcohol and cigarettes."

At his father's behest, Trump would sometimes take a few days off from his education and outside business activities to help his father out. One of those occasions was a rare instance when Fred Trump took a flyer on investing outside his Brooklyn/Staten Island fiefdom and bought the run-down Swiftton Village apartment complex in Cincinnati. In a story chronicling the history of the complex in *The Cincinnati Enquirer*, the building's long-time maintenance man, Roy Knight, would recall how Trump [the son] would, occasionally, come into town to supervise the restoration of the complex. "Donald Trump was not skilled," he said. "He often flew in for a few days at a time to help out with landscaping and other menial tasks."

Along the way, Trump did manage some informal, if not deep, friendships on campus, including several real estate professors who he considered his equal. And when he and his buddies would get into discussions, they rarely went to the news of the day but, most importantly, to the hot ladies on the Wharton campus. One coed that became hot on Trump's radar was Candace Bergen.

Born into a show business family, Bergen, who had already snagged important early roles in the films *The Group* and *The Sand Pebbles*, was taking a half - hearted flyer at higher education at the University of Pennsylvania and, while academically she was hanging on by a thread, she proved wildly popular, capturing the title of *Homecoming Queen* and *Miss University of Pennsylvania*. But while the consensus of opinion around campus was that Bergen was well beyond Trump, that did not stop her from noticing him around campus. "I had seen him around campus," she recalled in a 1992 speech at the university. "He was pretty hard to miss. He wore a two piece burgundy suit with matching burgundy patent leather boots."

Long story short, Trump did ask Bergen out. Bergen turned him down flat. But Trump took this rejection well. "She was so beautiful," he told *The Boston Globe*. "She was dating guys from Paris who were 35 years old. I did make the move. And I must say that she had the good sense to say 'Absolutely not.'"

Once again, how good a student Trump was during his years at Wharton remains a mystery of sorts to this day. But only a mystery depending on whom you talk to. There is nothing in research that indicates that Trump did not show up at class, do the required reading and assignments and did not contribute to class discussions. But did that translate into reaching the highest standards of academia by the time he graduated from Wharton in 1968?

According to Trump, who has never been shy about telling anyone who would listen how well he did at Wharton, it did…in a manner of speaking. "Let me tell you, I'm a really smart guy. I was a really good student at the best school in the country," he said on *Political Ticker. blogs. CNN*. In a 2004 conversation with *CNN*, he would continue to toot his own horn when it came to his achievements at Wharton. "I went to the Wharton School of Finance. I got very good marks. I was a good student."

In the book *Trump: The Saga of America's Most Powerful Real Estate Baron*, author Jerome Tuccille was quick to question Trump's dedication at Wharton. "He showed up for classes and did what was required of him but he was clearly bored and spent a lot of time on outside business activities."

Still the notion of Trump being an academic strongman during his years at Wharton continued in the public consciousness more than a half century after his graduation. A series of newspaper and magazine profiles, most notably *The New York Times*, continued to propagate the story that Trump was not only brilliant but had actually graduated from Wharton first in his class and with honors. Trump, for the record had, reportedly, never confirmed or denied that fact but his neutrality would keep that aspect of his public life front and center in people's minds. And over the years it would become a major bone of contention in both books and magazines.

In a 1984 *New York Times* magazine piece, William Geist revealed that Wharton commencement program from 1968 does not list Trump as graduating with honors of any kind. In a *The Daily News* piece, former Trump classmate at Wharton, Nancy Hano, was emphatic in stating, "He was not first in the class." The book *Trump: The Saga of America's Most Powerful Real Estate Baron*, takes a less piling on attitude, noting that Trump would later indicate that he had never made a statement about graduating first in class with honors at Wharton. *New York Magazine* would slap down the notion that Trump was a super intellect when, in a 1988 piece, it flatly stated that the idea that Trump had graduated first in class with honors 'was a myth.'

Bottom line, Trump did, in fact, graduate from Wharton in 1968 with a degree in economics, at which time he ran afoul of Uncle Sam. At that point, Trump's military deferments were officially over and he was suddenly faced with the prospect of being drafted. Trump's draft status would have, doubtless, never risen to anything but a minor footnote if it had not been for his 2015 verbal assault on John McCain in which he stated that the former POW should not be considered an American hero. The negative response to Trump's attack, not surprisingly, opened the floodgates to various news outlets suddenly looking into Trump's own lack of military service and how he managed to avoid it. Leading the mainstream media charge were the likes of *The National Review*, *The Washington Post* and *CBS News*. But if there was a media prize for the most thorough research, it would have to go to news gadfly *The Smoking Gun.com* who dug deep and came up with what most observers consider the definitive look into the lengths Trump went to avoid military service.

According to *The Smoking Gun.com*, Trump, after receiving two student deferments in1964 and 65, was, in late November 1966, briefly reclassified as 1-A, Available for Service. But within a few weeks, he was once again reclassified with a 2-S, student deferment. Trump would receive his final student deferment in Jan 1968, months before he graduated from Wharton.

The Smoking Gun's request for Trump's selective service records indicated that Trump was once again reclassified as 1-A. But much was a foot in Trump's world as, by October 15, 1968, he was, despite having gained a reputation as a physically superior specimen who had excelled in athletics throughout his life, had suddenly been reclassified as 1-Y (which would later be changed to a 4-F, unable to serve). The culprit? It turned out Trump had what were classified as bone spurs on the heels of both feet.

But Trump, suddenly in a situation where he had to dance around the McCain flap, brought into play the fact that he had actually gotten a high draft lottery number while still at Wharton in an interview with Fox affiliate television station *WNYW*.

"I actually got lucky because I had a very high draft number [356]," he said. "I was going to the Wharton School of Finance and I was watching as they did the draft numbers and I got a very, very high draft number and those numbers never got up to [called]"

It all made sense to Trump and, obviously, to those who would give him a pass on his memory. But the reality was that the very first draft lottery actually took place December 1, 1969…18 months after Trump graduated from Wharton, making his statement of being at school and watching the draft numbers either false or just a simple case of misremembering.

Chapter Five
Young Trump in the City

Trump left Wharton with a bachelor's degree in economics in 1968. He most likely felt in his gut that the degree was nothing more than a validation of what he had already learned through real world sweat equity, on the job training. According to his book *The Art of The Deal* and reported by *The Chicago Tribune*, the rookie entrepreneur already had a net worth of $200,000. Trump was anxious to get into the real estate game on a full time basis. And, he reasoned, what better place to start then at home?

What Trump discovered was that his father had, with age, evolved into an elder statesman, far from being a figurehead but slowly relinquishing much of the day to day running of the business to his wife Elizabeth and, by degrees during Trump's increasing participation during his college years, his son. Which was why, after Trump's literal return to the fold, the title of the company had morphed into *Elizabeth Trump & Son*.

Trump was immediately immersed into the day to day management of the mini empire which, after all the years, had continued to focus on middle class rental housing in his long held territories of Brooklyn, Queens and Staten Island. Trump eased into the working environment of his father but, within a year, was already growing restless at his father's extremely conservative philosophy that, while continuing to be successful, ultimately resulted in a limited vision and, predictably, smaller profit margins.

With the tacit approval of his father, Trump began to think outside the box according to an in-depth article in *The New York Times*. Trump began to move to the major leagues, buying properties in such alien (to his father) turf as Virginia, Ohio and Nevada and taking a gamble on the relatively cheap land prices in California.

But there was something more at work.

Any psychologist worth their salt would most likely have a field day dissecting the obvious Oedipal complex germinating between father and son. Trump was being driven by more than his business acumen. There was a barely hidden aggressive strain, an ego that was driving him to the big time and, yes, getting his name up in lights.

To his credit, Trump's father could see the handwriting on the wall. His son had the right instincts and attitudes for the business and would be the family member most likely to carry on the family's professional legacy. In 1971 Fred made it official when he turned over control of the business to his son. Donald immediately renamed the company *The Trump Organization*.

He took it all very seriously. Over the first couple of years under his stewardship, *The Trump Organization* continued to grow. But it was a slow and steady pace that continued to have Trump chomping at the bit. In 1971, Trump made the decision to move to Manhattan, the place he thought of as real estate Mecca, and prepare to move light years ahead.

Trump would concede in an *Evan Carmichael.com* piece that the move was born out of inner drive and ego. "I had loftier dreams and visions. And there was no way for me to implement them building housing in the outer boroughs of Queens."

Driven by status at this point, Trump had his eye on the glitz and glamour of the Upper East Side. The reality was that Trump could not afford much in that prized zip code. But, as he explained to *The Chicago Tribune*, he was quite content to get what he could.

"The turning point came in 1971 when I decided to rent a Manhattan apartment. It was a studio, in a building on Third Avenue and 57th Street and it looked out on a water tank. I was a kid from Queens who worked in Brooklyn and suddenly I had an apartment on the Upper East Side."

An apartment that, admittedly, was not up to Trump's real or imagined standards according to a piece in *NYU.EDU.com*. The story about Trump's early years indicated that it was a dated apartment in a very old building and that he had been reluctant to invite friends and family over to see it. But, for Trump, his new life in Manhattan had more to do with sweat equity than an Upper East Side address.

Although he was not hurting for money and, reportedly, he had his father's limo at his beck and call, Trump felt it was in his best interests to discover Manhattan, personally and professionally, on his feet; walking the city streets, taking in the sights and, most importantly to Trump, becoming aware of the surrounding buildings, their condition and, for his purposes, what was coming on the market and what might become a good investment.

But Trump knew that cultivating important social and professional contacts would be an important adjunct to his plans to mount a real estate career, which meant going where the super-rich and successful went which, in the early 70's. These included the ultra-exclusive *Le Club* where older, successful men would often be seen entering the club with as many as three women on their arms. Trump fit in quite well with the *Le Club* crowd as he would recall in *The Art of the Deal*.

"It turned out to be a great move for me socially and professionally. I met a lot of beautiful, single women and I went out almost every night. I never got involved with any of them very seriously. These were beautiful women, but many of them couldn't carry on a normal conversation."

With the onset of the disco era and its inherent heathenism, Trump moved deeper into the club scene in places like the infamous *Studio 54* where the up and coming real estate mogul would later admit to author Timothy O'Brien in the book *Trump Nation: The Art of Being the Donald* that he saw some amazing things. "I saw things happening there [*Studio 54*] that, to this day, I have never seen again. I would watch super models having sex, well-known super models having sex on a bench in the middle of a room. There were seven of them and each one was having sex with a different guy right in the middle of the room."

But while Trump was living the high life, he was also getting his feet wet in the high wire act that was the Big Apple's real estate market. When the Penn Central Railroad went into bankruptcy in 1973, Trump was quick to swoop in and obtain an option on the Penn Central Railroad yards, which he would ultimately resell for a big profit to the city of New York for the site for a convention center. He would also purchase the rights to a Penn Central hotel called The Commodore, refurbish it and eventually turn it into a profitable adjunct to Grand Central Station. In a matter of a couple of years, Trump, at the ripe old age of 27,was considered a rising star in the highly competitive Manhattan real estate universe. Things were looking up for Trump.

When suddenly his, and his father's, professional past came back to haunt him.

On October 16, 1973, *The New York Times* blasted a front-page headline story that stated that the Department of Justice had brought suit in federal court, charging Trump and his father (under the company name *Trump Management*)with violating the Fair Housing Act of 1968 in the operation of 39 buildings. In particular, the suit sited that *Trump Management* had refused to rent in the buildings in question because of race and color and that the company had required different rental terms and conditions based on race.

Trump's response to the charges? "They are absolutely ridiculous," he told *The New York Times*. "We never have discriminated and we never would."

Trump immediately took the offensive, hiring well-known firebrand lawyer, Roy M. Cohn, and countersuing the United States government on the grounds that the charges were "irresponsible and baseless" and designed to force *Trump Management* to rent to welfare recipients.

The legal system would grind on until June 1975 when a deal was struck that would allow qualified applicants of any race access to apartments in *Trump Management* properties. Trump was quick to note that the deal struck did not include any admission of guilt.

But, most likely, it was a sign to Trump that it was time to distance himself from his father's real estate empire and continue to create his own fortune on the streets of Manhattan. Trump was now 30 years old. Manhattan, in a space of three years had jump-started his net worth to a reported $200 million. He drove around in big cars and dated beautiful women. No one could doubt that Trump, figuratively and literally, had it all.

Except maybe Trump.

Chapter Six
Wife Number One

Trump had most certainly heard it all before. When was he going to settle down, get married and have lots of babies? His response could easily have been to gesture at his lifestyle, but he would often acknowledge that a more settled personal life had entered his thoughts, followed by the inevitable bromide that 'he had not met the right woman yet.'

On the surface, Ivana Marie Zeinickova (born February 20, 1949, in Czechoslovakia), would hardly have seemed to qualify as 'the right woman.' Trump would seem to have wanted a predictable, conservative woman in his life. Ivana seemed to be made of questions, unpredictability, intrigue and a bit too much mystery to be a sure thing.

A former child actress who had appeared in four Czech films, Ivana was a natural athlete who, under her father's tutelage, became quite the skier; reportedly so good that she was named as an alternative on the 1972 Czech Olympic Ski Team; a position that, according to *Spy Magazine*, would be extremely difficult to prove. Ivana would go on to gather a master's degree in physical education, while being temporarily engaged to a young film director, at Charles University in Prague. In 1971, Ivana married an Austrian skier named Alfred Winklmayr in order to obtain a foreign passport so that the reigning Communist leaders would not consider her a defector. Ivana would divorce Winklmayr in 1974 and would move to Canada the following year to be with her childhood friend, boutique owner George Syrovatka and did some modeling in Montreal. The nature of their relationship was maddeningly inconsistent. Several newspaper gossip items portrayed them as married. But when *Spy Magazine* began to dig some years later, all photo evidence had mysteriously disappeared. In any case, Ivana left Syrovatka after two years and immediately moved to New York to help promote the 1976 Montreal Olympics.

It was an odyssey that ended the night she meet Trump.

Ivana was at a public relations event at New York's swank *Maxwell's Plum* when, according to a thoroughly researched article in *Spy Magazine*, Trump spotted her from across the room. In an even more classic move, Trump sent a round of drinks over to her table. As they talked, Ivana found herself impressed but, at least initially, not overwhelmed with Trump. "I didn't get excited immediately," she said. "But it was Donald's energy that made him attractive." She would, years later, acknowledge on *The Oprah Winfrey Show*, "Donald always had a good head on his shoulders and I saw the potential."

Following that night, Ivana and Trump began a nine-month long distance relationship. A typical weekend would begin on a Friday with Ivana taking a plane from Montreal to New York where she would be met by Trump and his chauffeur-driven limo. Ivana's growing relationship would be a bit unorthodox, to say the least. Trump was always on the clock, with quiet dinners and romantic nights alone regularly interrupted by business calls that Trump just had to take. The reason being, while Trump was an up and comer in the New York real estate world, he was still the new kid on the block and was finding progress to be, often, rough.

Trump's ego and arrogance did not always mesh well with the more traditional and much older players in the real estate game. Trump's rubbing them the wrong way was rewarded with a lack of cooperation and withholding of the tricks of the trade when it came to negotiating deals and knowing the secrets of getting favorable rates, tax breaks and the inside track on currying favor with the city when it came to negotiating high end property deals. But through trial, error and a couple of major breakthrough deals, the door to the old boys' network in New York was finally swinging open...Just about the time Trump popped the question to Ivana.

The couple married on Easter Sunday, April 9, 1977 at the Marble Collegiate Church by Norman Vincent Peale while New York luminaries such as then-Mayor Beame and Roy Cohn were in attendance. It was a small, quiet and quite reserved ceremony attended by all the right people. In his book *Trump*, author Jerome Tuccille summed up Trump finding his soulmate in a very Trump-like manner, "Donald Trump had finally met a woman who had her head screwed on right."

Literally overnight Ivana found herself pregnant with the couple's first child, Donald Jr. (born December 31, 1977). And, most certainly, the months leading up to the birth were a time of reflection, both personally and speculatively, as the growing interest in the media wondered what kind of father Trump would be.

Trump would often acknowledge that much of his parenting skills were derived from his father. Fred was always working and so was not there for many of the important moments in his children's early years and Trump, on several occasions, would concede it would probably be the same with his own children. That Trump's children would be spoiled and given a sense of privilege in their lives was a given. That, like Trump, they would be given real world training and have it drummed into their heads that they would have to earn their quality of life would be a blueprint of what his father had taught Trump and his siblings.

Some years after the birth of Trump's first child, his parenting skills were called into question during a *20/20* television report that indicated that, amid all the nannies, the servants and Ivana, Trump actually spent only four to six hours of actual quality time a week with his children. During an interview on *The Oprah Winfrey Show*, Trump took the opportunity to address the 'quality time' issue when he quipped "I would say that I spend enough time with my children. I think they're covered."

But when it came to Trump's relationship with Ivana, it appeared that Trump had, indeed, found the ideal match. Truth be told, the ideal woman for Trump had always been somebody who would worship him in that old world, time honored way. And Ivana would admit, somewhat tongue in cheek in a *Women's Wear Daily* interview, that she was more than capable of domesticity. "My mother learned me everything. I can cook and I can press and I love to fuss around the house. I can take a shirt and I can press it and show the laundress just how Donald likes it."

Ivana had been a cultured, sophisticated learned woman. When they were out socially or in a business setting, she could be charming, able to hold her own in any conversation or setting and, finally, be the ideal woman on Trump's arm. Trump, most certainly, sensed that, while she would fulfill all her wifely and motherly duties in a somewhat traditional way (nannies and servants aside), she would not be denied her own thoughts and opinions. And early on in the marriage, Ivana's opinions were definitely important to Trump and his image.

When it came to Trump's wardrobe choices, the budding mogul was pretty much stuck in the pre-disco 70's, his fashion weapon of choice were plum-colored suits and matching boots. Not long after they met, Ivana sat Trump down and, not too subtlety, pointed him in the direction of pink, specifically pink shirts and ties. To her way of thinking, it was more 80's appropriate. For Trump, whose fashion choices always tended to lean toward that of a kid just out of college with not a whole lot of money, there was nothing he could say except, "That's the look."

Chapter Seven
Hits and Misses: The 80's

To say Trump was feeling his economic oats in the 1980's was an understatement. At a time when the US economy seemed good but not great and those who were getting paid to have the pulse on spending and saving were being cautious, Trump was seemingly hell-bent on living large and spending even larger, expanding his universe to bigger and bigger properties, an insurgent branding of Trump everything into progressive and even odd choices and seemingly walking a tightrope of unbridled wealth and daring the fates, and literally billions of dollars, to prove him wrong.

It was no accident that Trump would ultimately name his most successful and telling book *The Art of the Deal*, because in Trump's never-ending search for the bigger and better economic conquest, he really felt he was a Picasso or Rembrandt. "I love the creative process involved in the deal," he told *Playboy*. "I do what I do because of pure enjoyment. There's a beauty in making a great deal. It's my canvas and I like painting it."

Easily Trump's most opulent investment and, barring any acts of God, the most endearing legacy of

Trump's ego and economic largesse, is the Trump Tower in New York City. Construction began in 1980 on what would ultimately be a 58-story mixture of apartments, retail stores and an atrium on the site of the original Bonwit Teller store. The Trump Tower, upon its completion in 1983, would gain immediate cache among Big Apple residents for its sheer over-the-top elegance and a self-aggrandizing monument to Trump and all he believed himself to be.

But this being a Trump development, Trump Tower was not without its controversies and allegations that would, to this day, leave a bad taste in many people's mouths. Prior to the start of construction and at the not too subtle prodding of the architecture and arts community, Trump had agreed that much of the art deco statues and artistic grille work that adorned the Bonwit Teller building would be salvaged and donated to The Metropolitan Museum of Art. Unexpectedly, Trump had a change of heart once demolition of the original building began and, as documented in *The New York Times* and *The Cornell University Preservation News*, had the aesthetically irreplaceable works jack hammered into dust amid cries that Trump was thinking with his wallet rather than the promise he had made.

Trump's response, as noted in *The Preservation News*, did not help matters. He stated that the building artifacts he had destroyed "had no artistic merit," would have delayed construction of Trump Tower by ten days and would have cost Trump an additional $500,000.

Just as Trump Tower was set for its grand unveiling in '83, another dirty bit of business was uncovered when it was reported that 200 undocumented immigrants from Poland had been working off the books in the demolishing process, had been paid below-minimum wage wages, had been denied health and medical coverage and had been threatened with deportation if they complained. Trump's response during legal wranglings that would last nearly 15 years was that he rarely visited the demolition site and that a subcontractor had been responsible for the hiring of workers.

Gambling seemed to be in Trump's blood. To his way of thinking it must have, in his mind, walked hand in hand with the id and ego that seemed to drive him. It should not have come as a surprise when, in 1980, Trump announced that The Trump Plaza and Casino in Atlantic City, New Jersey, in a business partnership with Harrah's, was going into business as an upscale, decidedly high-roller mecca that would include 614 hotel rooms, seven restaurants, a glamorous entertainment showroom and a 60,000 square foot casino complex. It was not the best time for Trump to be getting into the gambling business, according to a story in *Casino Connection.com.*

Financing was getting harder to come by, interest rates were high and the advent and incursion of alternative forms of betting in the internet world, had already begun to take a financial bite out of traditional brick and mortar casinos. On the legal front, Trump had to jump through numerous hoops with the Casino Control Commission to get the all -important gambling licenses to open up shop. All of which combined to take four years before The Trump Plaza and Casino was up and running.

But for Trump, the casino gods would continue to make things difficult.

An hour after the official grand opening, a fire alarm went off, forcing the evacuation of the entire complex. It was also found that there were flaws in the slot machine accounting system, which, immediately, caused the shutdown of several traditionally lucrative gambling devices. To make matters worse, the earliest reports indicated that The Trump Plaza and Casino, while showing promise, opened at a sluggish seventh on the list of the top ten area casinos.

Part of the problem was a conflict between Trump and Harrah's, the later wanted to continue as a middle market, low-level gambling outlet while Trump was dead set on going high end, high-roller at all costs. Within five months of the opening, Trump had bought out Harrah's and, over the next decade would be free to spend his own money on expanding the property and, essentially, spending more money than he was making. But Trump was persistent, fighting off the occasional lawsuit and continuing to pour more money and try the patience of investors before ultimately selling his interest in the property some 25 years later.

Trump's mania to turn a buck and to further the branding of his name in every possible corner of the planet would, occasionally, veer off into la la land, investments seemingly fueled more by vanity than sound economic sense. Two of those missteps were chronicled in *Time Magazine*.

In 1988, Trump decided he wanted to get into the commercial airline business and bought out a small passenger shuttle company called Eastern Air Shuttle. For a reported $365 million, Trump was given 17

Boeing 727 airplanes, the rights to land and take off from east coast airports in Boston, New York and Washington D.C. and the rights to rename the company Trump Airlines and plaster his name on the fuselage of the planes. Once again, Trump was thinking beyond just running a no frills puddle jumper which Eastern had been. Trump wanted luxury and to that extent, added such glamorous items as chrome seat belt latches, gold colored bathroom fixtures and maple wood veneer on the floors. The enterprise would be a total bust, with passengers more interested in a cheap rather than a high rolling ride. The fact that fuel prices had taken that moment to jump sky high did not help matters either. For Trump, this was a particularly stinging defeat. He was forced to default on his loans and ownership of Trump Airlines was turned over to his creditors. Trump Airlines ceased to exist in 1992.

The little kid in Trump surfaced in 1989 when he teamed up with board game giant Milton Bradley to put out a Monopoly-style game called *Trump: The Game*. In typical Trump fashion, Trump was all over the media, trumpeting *Trump: The Game* as a can't-miss smash that would, doubtless, sell two million units in a year. One year later, the game was a dismal failure and promptly disappeared off shelves and, most certainly, into a warehouse where they await the possible resurrection as a collector's item.

Trump's sporting nature came to the fore in 1983 when he threw his considerable fortune behind the New Jersey Generals one of the initial entries in the upstart United States Football League. It would be a short-lived venture as Trump, for some unknown reason, sold the franchise to oil magnate J. Walter Duncan who, in turn, sold it back to Trump in 1984. Trump took an active advocacy role in the new pro league, even, at one point, suggesting that the USFL go head to head with the National Football League. But the kind of combat Trump liked never came to pass as the USFL, not surprisingly, ran into financial problems and folded in 1986.

However Trump's instincts and strengths continued to be the mogul's finest hours during the 80's, especially when he thought ahead of the curve. In 1983, Trump Parc was a dated and somewhat tumbled down building next to Central Park South. Central Park did not have the most sterling reputation at the time, but Trump sensed its current reputation as a hotbed of crime was turning upward as more and more people were flocking to New York. Consequently more than one money maven looked askance when Trump paid $13 million for the questionable property. But Trump would have the last laugh when, after tearing down the property and reconfiguring it into condominiums, he watched as Trump Parc caught the uptick in real estate and, by 1988, total sales of condos in the building had risen to $250 million.

When it came to adding casinos to his portfolio, Trump had seemingly not learned his lesson with his up and down history with the casino in Atlantic City. In 1988, Trump, in a mammoth three way deal that also included another big player, Merv Griffin and Resorts International, in which Trump would get the Taj Mahal Casino while Griffin took the remainder of the assets from *Resorts International*. Needless to say, Trump, in a story in *The New York Times*, was thrilled with the deal. "He [Griffin] paid me a fortune and I got the crown jewel. Beating Merv was a lot of fun."

But Trump's joy at the purchase would be short lived.

Less than a year after the purchase, Trump once again hit troubled financial days and, amid mounting debt, was unable to meet his loan payments to investors. In fact things were so dire that Trump was forced into bankruptcy. Bankruptcy was a bitter pill for Trump to swallow, but through his knowledge of how the game was played, Trump was able to soften the blow when he came to an agreement with bondholders. Trump was not used to eating crow and it was, most likely, a huge blow to his ego. But he gritted his teeth as he worked out a deal with bondholders who had already lost millions while backing Trump's latest purchase.

When the dust settled, Trump agreed to give up 50% of his ownership rights to the Taj Mahal to the bondholders in exchange for lower interest rates on the debt and more time to pay off the loan on the debt. Easily one of the most satisfying purchases of the 80's would turn out to be his 1988 purchase of the opulent Plaza Hotel. Given his erratic history of high end purchases that had not caused some kind of emotional or financial headache, many observers of all things Trump would have guessed that the free-spending real estate and branding-mogul would have pulled in his horns a bit at the prospect of yet another high end deal. But, as reported in *The New York Times*, Trump willingly laid down $400 million to purchase The Plaza Hotel. In the spirit of keeping things in the family, Trump appointed his wife, Ivana, President of

The Plaza who would be in charge, after running everything by her husband, of the day to day running and upkeep of his latest purchase.

Trump would joke about putting his wife in the seat of power with *The New York Times*. "I gave Ivana a salary of $1 a year and all the dresses she can buy."

But it would emerge some years later that the seemingly playful appointment had a much more sinister core. It would emerge that Trump and Ivana's marriage was in the early stages of dissolution. It was reported in an in-depth *Vanity Fair* piece that Trump and Ivana were, by the mid 80's, living in separate apartments of the palace-like Trump Tower and that Trump, in his first real bout of financial problems, resulting in sales of such high priced toys as the Trump yacht, had taken to Howard Hughes style solitude, subsisting on junk food and those who saw him during this period observed that he did not look well.

Consequently, Ivana was willing to spill the beans to *Vanity Fair* about the truth behind her appointment. "Donald said 'you act like my wife and come back to New York [to manage The Plaza Hotel] and take care of your children or you can run the casino in Atlantic City and we get divorced.'"

"What am I going to do? If I don't do what he says, I'm going to lose him."

Chapter Eight
Trump Takes New York

Trump's business acumen during the 80's would, more often than not, consist of equal parts bragging and guile, with no small measure of cocksureness. It was a combination that often rubbed his peers and competitors the wrong way. Many were secretly hoping that Trump would fall flat on his face. But Trump was proving a miracle worker when it came to business in New York.

Trump was no angel, although he would often project an air of charity and good works. By the mid 80's, he was rounding out a series of successful and profitable ventures with the completion of a series of lavish yet relatively cheap residences in the long-neglected and under- appreciated Central Park South area. One fly in the aesthetic ointment was that the completed complex had a fairly unobstructed view of a New York White Elephant called The Wollman Ice Skating Rink.

The rink had been an eyesore for some years according to a report by *Philly.com*. The city was at wits end. Six years of bungled attempts at renovating the dormant but beloved rink had put the city of New

York more than $12 million over budget with no end to the project in sight. Whether Trump's interest in the crumbling, rusty hulk was charity or improving the view from his just completed Central Park project is not certain. But what is known is that Trump stepped in with an offer the city could not refuse.

"Just give the project to me," Trump said to Philly.com, in a quote dating back to June 1986. "I'll finish the rink by Christmas. This Christmas. And I'll do it for free. I have total confidence that we will be able to do it."

New York City had nothing to lose at this point and so the City gave Trump the go ahead. Reportedly, Trump had the advantage of being an independent developer and so could avoid a lot of hurdles that big cities had to negotiate and inevitably delayed projects like The Wollman Rink. That Trump was willing to take on the project out of his own pocket most certainly cut through a lot of red tape.

By late October 1986, Trump had not only completed The Wollman Ice Skating Rink two months ahead of schedule but also had managed to undercut his own costs by an estimated $750,000. Trump boasted of his development triumph in a speech at the official unveiling in November (reported by Philly.com) that, "This serves as an example of what New York, the wealthiest city in the world, can do in terms of saving money."

Trump coppered an obviously ego-driven success by hiring The Ice Capades to oversee the day-to-day operation of The Wollman Rink and offered to operate the rink for a period of one year, with any profits from his tenure at the top going to charity. By April 1987, as reported by *The New York Times*, it was announced that The Wolman Ice Skating Rink had turned an estimated profit between $500,000 and $1.5 million.

Already well known for his daring in development and real estate deals throughout the 80's, Trump's aggressive style would continue, seemingly unabated, into the next decade as a literal Svengali who, figuratively and literally, ran on instinct and perception and put potential consequences and downfalls in his mental rear view mirror.

A perfect example of this bravado was his 1990's acquisition of what was considered the prime, trophy building in midtown Manhattan, the General Motors Building. Over the years, Trump had been drawn to the potential of the midtown area, having gobbled up properties that would ultimately become Trump Tower and Trump International Hotel and Tower. That he would take a flyer on yet another midtown property that would, most likely, be hotly contested and run into the hundreds of millions of dollars was the kind of enticement that appealed to Trump in a way that much of his 80's financial conquests had.

"It's already a premiere building," Trump assessed to *The New York Times*. "But it can be greatly enhanced."

Trump sat quietly on the sidelines as the expected bids rained down. Then in what seemed like the last possible minute, he swooped in and closed the deal on the GM Building for a reported $800 million bid, $40 million of which would serve as the down payment. Many were amazed at Trump's stealthy tactics. John Mechanic, a real estate lawyer involved in the transaction, was among them.

"It's a little surprising that an entrepreneur ended up in a bidding contest like that as the high bidder," he told *The New York Times*. "I guess ego would probably have something to do with it."

But as Trump would acknowledge to *The New York Times* in the aftermath of his latest victory, it all made good business sense. The General Motors Building was already 98 % leased. Trump was not concerned. A great many of the leases would come due in the next four or five years and he would increase the rents substantially.

"Some of the leases would be doubled or even quadrupled," he predicted.

And like all of Trump's acquisitions, it all seemed to make good business sense.

Chapter Nine
Trouble in Paradise

The novelty of presiding over one of her husband's biggest purchases was a double-edged sword for Ivana. She enjoyed having a position of power and those around her would often admit that she was serious and quite good at it.

But with the birth of Ivanka (October 30, 1981) and Eric (January 6, 1984),Ivana's motherly instincts kicked in. Heading up the Taj Mahal Casino was suddenly not as important as spending quality time with her children and she told Trump as much. As reported in *Bio.com* and several other outlets, Trump seemed anxious to keep his wife in the working world and so she reluctantly accepted his counter offer, President of another Trump property, The Manhattan Plaza. A reluctance that, by the mid 80's, saw the Trump marriage on shaky ground. Reportedly the couple were arguing a lot more and, to those who saw them out and about, including a *Vanity Fair* writer, there was an obvious distance between them. Those who knew them well could see that they were going through great pains to keep up the illusion of the love they had felt early on in the marriage.

Add the seemingly countless business trips Trump was taking and it was inevitable that the gossip columns and tabloid press were regularly abuzz with alleged extramarital affairs Trump was either having or had reportedly had with a who's who of the celebrity and business world. Among those taking their turn as 'the other woman' were actress Catherine Oxenberg, boxer Mike Tyson's wife Robin Givens, model Carol Alt, former Olympic skating champion Peggy Fleming, cosmetics executive Georgette Mosbacher and designer Carolyne Roehm. Trump was having a good laugh at the notion that he was sleeping with every woman on the planet in a conversation with *People*. "I see the names of women I was supposed to have slept with. They named two that I've never met, two others that I shook hands with. Then they named Robyn Givens. Would I want her then husband Mike Tyson after me?

A very real problem was now that Trump was constantly manic for the next big deal, seemingly always out of town, playing the often necessary political games that went hand in hand with the real estate business and a, likewise, constant drive for self-promotion that had kept their marriage and their lives always in the public eye.

That Trump was aware of what was going on in his marriage and of his obsession was made evident years later when he, candidly, talked about both with *Nightline*. "I know it's very hard for them [his ex-wives] to compete because I love what I do. I do. I really love it."

Around the time of their next child's birth, the rumors began to circulate that many of Trump's out of town work trips were involving clandestine meetings with other women. As it would turn out, one of those 'alleged' affairs turned out to be real.

Marla Maples had been a fairly big fish in an almost stereotypical Georgia pond. A Southern Belle with down-home charm and beauty to die for, Marla seemed destined for bigger and better things and, by the time she turned 18, she appeared to be on the right track. From high school prom queen to small parts in commercials and low budget films and finally to New York, where she lived out her hopes and dreams on The Great White Way from the confines of a $400 a month studio apartment. It was in 1985 that Marla met Trump at a celebrity tennis tournament in Atlantic City.

"We knew we had this connection," Marla recalled to *New York Magazine* some three decades later. "I knew I truly loved this guy."

But the consensus among media observers was that Trump was thinking with his little head and not his heart. Trump's seduction was pretty much by an age-old blueprint. He told Marla that his marriage to Ivana was not good and that plans were in place to divorce her soon. Marla recalled in *New York Magazine* that they would spend hours on the phone but, for the first three years of the affair, they were never seen out in public.

"I loved this man," Marla said. "Yes, I was young but it was my choice. I was romanced. I had Mr. Charm all over me and it was very hard to say no."

Trump's prowess in the boardroom also apparently extended to the bedroom. At least that's what Marla had people believe in 1991 when she was quoted in big bold headlines in *The New York Post* as saying "Sex with Donald Trump was the best sex I ever had." Some years later Marla, in conversation with *Access Hollywood*, was a little vague on the matter. "I think Donald had the opportunity to go to the papers and he chose not to. Did I ever say it? Well I don't want to destroy him. Maybe I whispered it along the way but it was not meant for public domain."

Trump immediately began to take a professional as well as personal interest in Marla. He was always there with suggestions about her career, at one point even putting himself in charge of selecting her press photos. He even strongly suggested, as revealed in *The Sun Sentinel*, that Marla accept a one million dollar offer to pose nude in *Playboy* and even went so far as to get on the phone with the magazine to broker the deal. Ultimately Marla decided against the offer, stating in *The Sun Sentinel* piece that, "I'm thankful for my body but I didn't want to exploit it."

The clandestine relationship between Trump and Marla would continue through 1988, with the couple often getting together under the nose of Ivana and the family. In one instance, as described by *Vanity Fair*, Trump's oldest son ran into his father and Marla at an Elton John concert. In another instance, described in a *People* article about Trump and his revolving relationships, Trump, reportedly, managed to find time to sneak away from his family during attendance at a church service to be with Marla. Eventually a picture of Marla as the 'other woman' and in a relationship with the very-married Trump, made the infamous Page Six column of *The New York Post* and the secret was out.

Ivana was fuming and immediately confronted Trump who danced around the question but ultimately confessed. The marriage was indeed on the rocks and hanging by the proverbial thread. But the couple continued to try to put the best face on a situation that was rapidly turning into a media feeding frenzy.

On December 29, 1989, Trump and Ivana, on a Christmas skiing holiday in Aspen, Colorado, which was punctuated by constant arguments and accusations, had the occasion to confront Marla, who coincidentally also happened to be in Aspen and staying at the same resort. According to gossip columnist Liz Smith, who pulled no punches, Ivana screamed, "You bitch! Leave my husband alone!" Trump, who was sitting within earshot of the blow up, hopped on his skis and beat a hasty retreat down the mountainside with Ivana hot on his heels. It was comic as well as tragic and everybody came out looking bad, especially Trump.

In a *People* article chronicling the showdown, Marla told Ivana that she was in love with her husband. Decades later, Marla would relive that moment with *New York Magazine*. "It was just a moment of us both wanting to know the truth. It was good that the truth became known, but that was also when the real pain began. I realized that we had both been deceived."

Evidence of Trump's two timing both women became laughable when, as reported by both *Shagtree.com* and *Who Dated Who?.com*, while cheating on Ivana with Marla, Trump, through a good part of 1989, had also, allegedly, been seeing tennis star Gabriella Sabatini.

Marla choose to lay low in the face of this public humiliation while Trump, conveniently, had a business trip to Japan to go to; also on the agenda was watching good friend Mike Tyson fight. But for Ivana, it was the last straw. Midway through February 1990, Ivana announced that she was divorcing Trump.

When Trump returned from his trip to Japan, he was bombarded with lawyers lining up to handle the impending divorce case and reporters wanting his side of the story. Trump resorted to platitudes when addressing the issue with *People*, seemingly clueless to the notion that his infidelities might have had something to do with the breakup of the marriage. "I love my children and I will always love Ivana," he said. "Right now our paths have gone in different directions. But I would never do anything to hurt her. Ivana is a good woman. But you grow apart. People understand that."

Trump would insist that the divorce would be amicable and quick. His confidence on that front may well have had something to do with both prenuptial and post-nuptial agreements that Ivana had signed prior to the start of their 12-year marriages. What she would receive for the sweat equity put into the marriage was custody of the couple's three children, the $3.7 million Greenwich, Connecticut home and a $25 million cash settlement. Sound good? To most of the living, breathing world it would have been fine.

But Ivana was not like most of us. At least she did not think so. Through her lawyers, Ivana argued that, at the time, Trump was reportedly worth $1.7 billion and that $25 million was estimated at only 1.5 percent of Trump's net worth. She fired back with a counter offer; sole ownership of *The Plaza Hotel* and a $150 million cash settlement. Trump was not happy at all but he played it cool in a statement to *People* in which he said, quite simply, "The prenuptial agreement is airtight."

Over the remainder of 1990, the Donald/Ivana divorce was front-page news, a three-ring circus of gossip, innuendo and borderline slander as the feuding Trumps, often on the record and very much in the public eye, became a daily soap opera. One which was fueled by Trump's now freedom to be seen out and about with Marla. But to what degree Trump was flaunting his new romantic life was always open to conjecture.

To a large extent, Trump had seemed to have gone underground, largely spotted on his way to or from his office or a business meeting. Because the reality was that times were tough, even for a Donald Trump, and he had to continue to make money if, for no other reason, than to feed his massive drive and ego. The sightings of Trump and Marla together, by comparison, were rare and fleeting. When Trump was cornered for a comment on his divorce proceedings, he would usually dismiss questions with a brisk quip or one liner. One could sense that Trump saw the divorce was more of a petty annoyance, akin to swatting a fly. If he was truly upset at being the center of attention for what he considered all the wrong reasons, he was not showing it.

Finally, late in March 1991 as reported by *Newsday, The Baltimore Sun* and other news outlets, the Trumps, after a marathon session that lasted well past midnight, settled their differences and a legal, binding divorce decree was announced. It had been testy to the bitter end with the pair fighting over ownership of a Mercedes which, argued Ivana, Trump had given her and then, subsequently, repossessed. At the end of the day, Ivana got the Mercedes back as well as $14 million in cash ($10 million at the settlement hearing and $4 million contingent upon her vacating the Trump Tower building), $300,000 annually in child support and $350,000 a year in alimony, the 45-room Greenwich, Connecticut mansion and use of Trump's Florida mansion for one month out of the calendar year. Both sides seemed happy and relieved at the decision but Trump, never one to relinquish the last word, said in the *Newsday* report after the decision was rendered…

"She had been nickel and diming me over the car."

Chapter Ten
More of the Same

Trump hates the B word: Bankruptcy. He's been asked about it for years, but once he gets over fuming over the asking of the question, he can be quite logical and persuasive in explaining how Bankruptcy for the very wealthy and influential is really no big deal, as was the case in a conversation with *ABC News*.

"I've used the laws of this country to pare debt," Trump explained. "We'll have a company, we'll throw it into a chapter. We'll negotiate with the banks and make a fantastic deal. It's not personal. It's just business."

According to *Forbes*, which took a good look at Trump's early 90's financial falls, the Chapter 11 surrounding Trump's Taj Mahal Casino, was, brought about because of the mogul's inability to make payments to investors on their loans, was settled formally and without much rancor. Trump gave up 50% of the ownership in the casino to investors in exchange for a lower interest rate and more time to repay the loan. But it was safe to say that Trump's money stumble, in 1992, over another failure to pay his financial obligations to lenders in the Trump Plaza

Hotel, dug a bit deeper, 49% of ownership in the hotel went to Citibank and five other investors. But what must have struck at Trump's ego was that, while he would maintain the title of Chief Executive to The Plaza Hotel, he would not be paid for the job title and would have no role in the day-to-day operations of the hotel. Consequently, the concept of 'just business' had reduced Trump to a figurative puppet.

But Trump did not emerge a pauper. His meat and potato real estate properties as well as the branding of the Trump name on other projects still made him a very rich man. But dealing with the consequences of debt still hurt, especially being fresh off a very expensive divorce from Ivana. He was certainly not in the ideal state of mind to enter the next phase of his personal life with Marla Maples.

But that was exactly where he was heading. Whether it was love or lust, Trump and Marla were seemingly joined at the hip when out in public and in the paparazzi viewfinder. But if the stories appearing in the tabloids and the celebrity press were any indication, the road to any alter would be rocky indeed. Shortly after being officially set free from Ivana, Trump presented Marla with a $15,000 friendship ring. But while the ring represented togetherness, it did not necessarily mean fidelity.

Not long after Marla got the ring, the gossip and tabloid outlets were alive with stories of Trump being out, about and cozy with several other women. Marla cut off all contact with Trump but the pair would get back together a few days later, with Marla reportedly sporting a monster of an engagement ring and, as reported in *The New York Times* and *The Daily News*, a wedding date for later in the year. A date that by July 1991 was cancelled. Trump acknowledged the cancellation with *The Daily News* when he said, "I want to remain friends with her but it's time to step aside and look in other directions."

Trump's remark was considered vintage Trump. He did not want to be married and ultimately wanted what was best for Trump. Once again nobody spoke for a while but, eventually, they got back together, got serious once again about getting married and began arguing about something that was very near and dear to Trump's heart. The Pre-nup. Marla was an old-fashioned girl who only thought of marriage in the purest, spiritual sense. Trump, fresh off giving a big chunk of money to Ivana, coupled with persistent rumors that he had been the latest victim of the junk bond fiasco and easy bank loans and was now reportedly $1 billion in debt, was not about to make another matrimonial mistake. Consequently, over the next year, the rollercoaster ride that was Trump and Marla became a media spectator sport. Five times wedding plans would be announced and, just as quickly, cancelled. The relationship seemed headed for disaster.

Until early in 1993, when Marla announced that she was pregnant.

Trump was reportedly thrilled at the news. He had come from a large family and had often proclaimed that he wanted the same for himself. But there was that old devil pre-nup standing in the way and Trump continued to hold out until Marla gave him the ultimatum...Marriage or she was gone. Trump was caught in the middle. Short of running down to city hall and getting a quickie marriage, in advance of the birth of his child with Marla, Trump was seemingly trapped and teetering on a marriage that most considered more lust than love. But on October 13, 1993, with the birth of a daughter named Tiffany, Trump, at least for the moment, was the ideal proud father, genuinely (at least in the public eye) happy and warm and seemingly in the perfect state of mind to make everything with Marla legal and binding.

On December 21, 1993, Trump and Marla exchanged vows at The Plaza Hotel. Marla had hoped that their marriage could be a little more intimate but knew what she was getting into, which was wide open and flamboyant. More than a thousand guests, both in and out of Trump's business realm, rubbed shoulders with the invited press that included 17 television crews, 90 paparazzi and hordes of newspaper reporters and gossip columnists. Trump and his new bride mixed and mingled easily with the assembled throng, posing for pictures and, according to the countless media reports, appeared happy and very much in love.

Among those present was Trump's good friend radio shock jock Howard Stern who, at one point, was heard to say, "This maybe in bad taste but I give the marriage four months."

Trump seemed in a mind to make this work. But far away from the festivities, in an office, in a safe, a pre-nuptial agreement, signed by Marla, sat in silent repose.

Marla was hoping for the good life. What she got was the Trump life.

The newly married couple maintained a residence in New York but made Trump's long standing home in

Florida their main home. Marla was enthralled with the sheer grandeur of the Mar-a-Lago home and was looking forward to transforming it into a storybook family retreat. What she had not counted on was that her husband, in a seemingly never-ending search for money, had decided to turn his home into a glorified country club for the rich and famous. Consequently Mar-a-Lago was soon open to whoever could pay a $75,000 initiation fee and $6,000 a month rent. Reportedly Michael Jackson had spent some time there, but one thing was certain: Marla and Trump were never alone. Parties, in Florida and New York, always seemed to have a cast of hundreds while Marla would often, as explained in *People*, hope against hope for a simple and private dinner for two.

Trump, according to various reports, was a good husband and father but, much like his father had been, was always consumed by business and often unavailable and neglectful emotionally. He always seemed to be out of town on business. For her part, Marla always wanted to experience life, to go places and do things. But on those occasions when they would travel to Europe or some other seemingly idyllic place, it quickly became evident that, for Trump, it was just a business trip and that she would have to fend for herself much of the time.

By the mid 90's, Trump's always-manic pursuit of millions, most likely, was in response to media scrutiny into just how much he was actually worth. Still suffering shell shock from the previous bankruptcies, Trump, as reported in several business articles from the likes of *Money* and the book *Trump Nation*, indicated that Trump's investments had suddenly turned extremely conservative and, while they indicated he was far from being a pauper, he was also not the billionaire his cultivated public persona would lead people to believe. Trump was becoming extremely paranoid at the intrusion; often threatening lawsuits at the mere mention of Trump as only a millionaire and not a billionaire.

It was the rare interview during this time that Trump did not manage to let drop how much everything he owned cost, an example being when *ABC News* did what was essentially a puff profile on Trump that included a tour of his private plane. At one point, Trump pointed out a high-end piece of artwork hanging on one of the walls and, typically Trump, he glossed over the virtues of the artist and the aesthetics of the work and proudly pointed out that the painting had cost him ten million. In Trump's mind, the only thing that was important was the cost and his ability to buy it.

The consensus among many observers was that Trump, now closing in on age 50, was still a very immature man. His ego-driven attitudes were nothing new, nor was his abrupt way of doing business that, alternately, was attractive and off putting. It was part and parcel of a caricature, cultivated by Trump and embraced by the media, that had been fun to explore in a bigger than life way. But, by the mid 90's, Trump's persona was beginning to get tiresome and those coming in contact with him were beginning to take a tougher look.

One person who took dead aim at Trump during this period was author/journalist Mark Bowden who, in the mid 90's, had been commissioned by *Playboy*

Magazine to do a profile on Trump. Trump had always imagined himself a *Playboy* kind of guy and so he willingly opened the doors to his Florida home and family. Bowden did his due diligence and the *Playboy* piece was quite good. But the author was not finished with Trump. In a follow up of sorts in *Vanity Fair*, he took a personal look at Trump and found much in his subject that was distasteful.

In the piece, he saw Trump as a "vain man trying to make a good impression," and was prone to telling stories that, upon further examination "were not true."He pictured Trump as somebody who ran roughshod over those working for him. Trump, in Bowden's view, "was somebody who had turned 50 and was not too happy about it." The tone of the *Vanity Fair* piece painted a picture of a man of wealth who may well have been teetering on the precipice of being relevant and desperate to prove he was by any means necessary. At one point, Bowden reported that Trump, sensing a story that would not paint him in the best light, attempted a not too subtle bribe when he hinted that he was going to need a writer for his next book and wondered if Bowden was interested? Bowden refused as he was already on to the work that would make him very well known, the book *Black Hawk Down.*

Marla came across in the story as polite and sarcastically condescending. A sure sign to Bowden that their marriage, by then going on six years, was in decline. But not necessarily for the reason that many suspected. Trump's ego, the constant emphasis on doing as much business and making as much money as possible, as well as the difference in lifestyle and spiritual attitudes, were the obvious culprits; as was Trump's seeming financial problems.

Adding to the speculation were several reports that Trump had been cheating on Marla during their marriage. However, Marla was the first to state in *AZ quotes.com* that Trump had never cheated on her during their marriage. But in a quote in *People Magazine* attributed to an unnamed source, Trump had reportedly told close confidants that, "one of his major challenges in life was handling challenges from women. If you get hit on one hundred times, it's tough to go home to Marla and say, 'Hi, how you doing?'" Infidelity was a question that never seemed to go away and, given Trump's dubious track record, it all seemed to make sense

As it would turn out, what finally put the final nail in the Trump/Marla marriage may well have been an alleged affair, not by Trump but, rather, indirectly, by Marla. In April 1996, *The National Enquirer* and countless other outlets including *The Orlando Sentinel* ran with the story that Florida police had come upon Marla and one of Trump's bodyguards, one Spencer Wagner, in a secluded area 12 miles from the Trump estate. Marla was quoted in *The Orlando Sentinel* as saying the whole incident was innocent and that the bodyguard was merely standing guard nearby while Marla took an unplanned bathroom break.

Marla would dismiss the story with contempt in *The Orlando Sentinel* when she said, "our life is so full of love. I don't have time for this." For his part, Trump would angrily discount the story with one word "despicable."

It seemed innocent enough but Trump, as it would be later revealed in *People*, would secretly use his connections to check out Marla's story, which he would determine was true and that there was no hanky-panky going on. Those close to Trump would indicate off the record in *People* that Trump might well have used his vetting of the incident as a litmus test of his wife's fidelity. And, for the moment, it appeared that Marla had passed with flying colors.

But by all accounts, Trump's massive ego had taken a major psychological hit in the aftermath of the incident, one he reportedly would never completely recover from. It was at that point that Trump, figuratively and literally, took the prenuptial agreement out of his safe. Based on the particulars of the agreement both Marla and he had signed, Marla, should they divorce, would be entitled to between one and five million dollars. Always looking at the bottom line, Trump saw that if he stayed married to Marla for much longer, she would be entitled to the higher amount.

Trump and Marla separated in mid-1997. All the reports indicated that the split was amicable and, as reported in *E Online.com* and other media outlets, was complete with a joint statement that read: "After a long relationship and three and a half years of marriage, we have decided to separate as friends." Marla, in a quote from *Inspirational Quotes About Life.com* seemed to reinforce what was looking like an amicable split when she said, "When we separated I did not want this to turn into a slugfest and so I decided to take the high road."

But when Trump's lawyer filed divorce papers three months after the separation, the high road suddenly turned bumpy. Trump's initial payout to Marla was reportedly in the neighborhood of $2 million. But, with the untold millions first wife Ivana had received. and the reality that Trump was, at the time, allegedly worth in excess of a billion, Marla, legal team in hand, began fighting for more, much more, with reportedly figures hovering in the vicinity of $25 million being tossed around. Trump's response was that the pre-nup was ironclad. And so while the lawyers continued to haggle over millions, Trump and Marla went their separate ways.

Trump remained largely silent as the divorce proceedings lumbered through the courts. Marla, on the other hand, was upfront in lamenting the dissolution of the marriage with *Contactmusic.com* "The money made it hard for me and Donald to have the time for a relationship. It was very difficult to work on us and the marriage."

Trump was not going to let a little thing like not being legally divorced get in the way of his resuming his pursuit of the ladies. In 1998 he briefly dated well-known model/actress/ entrepreneur Kara Young. It was also during this period that Trump made headlines when he attempted to get up close and personal with the newly divorced Princess Diana.

Although it has never been clear how and when Trump met Diana, Trump would insist in his 1997 book, *The Art of The Comeback* that "I met her on a number of occasions. She was a genuine princess. A dream lady." A Trump spokesman, quoted in the *British Sunday Times* and, subsequently, *USA Today* indicated, "Trump and Diana had a great relationship and liked each other a lot. But nothing ever came of it."

Selina Scott, a UK television journalist and a confidant of the late Diana, told the *British Sunday*

Times a different story. "He [Trump] bombarded Diana with massive bouquets of flowers, each worth hundreds of pounds. Trump clearly saw Diana as the ultimate trophy wife. Diana said 'What am I going to do? He gives me the creeps.' I told her to just throw them [the flowers] in the bin."

The divorce became final in February 1999. Marla had reportedly grown tired of the growing acrimony surrounding the marriage and the relationship that had become the red meat for the gossip and tabloid press and finally agreed to the terms of the prenuptial agreement. For her years with Trump, Marla walked away with a bit over $2 million and primary custody of their daughter Tiffany. Trump was magnanimous in his post settlement comments, acknowledging that his daughter with Marla would always be taken care of. But Trump showed he could continue to play hardball with Marla, post-divorce, when Marla signed a deal with publisher Harper Collins to write a tell-all book about Trump tentatively titled *All That Glitters Is Not Gold.* The book was abandoned when Trump threatened to sue on the grounds that the book violated the terms of the divorce agreement.

In the aftermath of the divorce, Trump's financial status, at least in the eyes of the public, had started to look up thanks to judicious branding and a mixture of conservative and ego-driven projects. The consensus was that Trump's net worth by 1999 was well into the billions (a situation Trump had insisted was the case all along). It was a situation that, no doubt, was helped with the death of Trump's father in June 1999. At the time of his death, Frank Trump's net worth was reported to be worth in the neighborhood of $300 million and the terms of the will was that the estate would be split between all of his children, essentially adding an estimated $70 million to the Trump coffers.

But while Trump was never far from the next big deal and the next money making venture, he actually had other things on his mind. Trump, depending on how one looked at it, was once again actively on the prowl for lust and love, preferably both and, by 1998, had reportedly found both in the latest love of his life, Melania Knauss.

Chapter Eleven
Third Time's the Charm

Trump had never given the impression that he was in a hurry to get married and, following his divorce from Marla, seemed quite content. But, in his private moments, he would often play up the importance of family and, as he aged, insisted that even with four children, there was still a desire to enlarge his brood. Trump would often insist that a future wife at this point would have to have her own mind and her own drive, ambitions and attitudes, perhaps with an unintentional aside to first wife Ivana. Many cynics rolled their eyes at those pronouncements, because the reality, truth be known, was that Trump had always gravitated toward a nice, somewhat submissive woman who deferred to him in all instances. Trump, as many would acknowledge, was always enamored of the concept of 'the trophy wife.'

And in Melania Knauss, Trump seemed to have found his latest dream woman.

Melania (born April 26, 1970 in Slovenia) was, from the beginning, far from the traditional European stereotype. She was inquisitive, always striving to learn and, in her own way, a driven go-getter, much in the way of Trump. Design and architecture were her courses of choice at university. After graduation she gravitated toward the high glitz of modeling where her soft but striking good looks made her a regular on the fashion runways of Milan and Paris. By 1996, Melania was seeking new experiences in the United States, where she mixed with fashion photographers and made her way to the cover of several high-end magazines.

She mingled with all the right people at all the right parties where she was, by media observers, a star on the rise. It was at one such party in 1998 that Melania met Trump. In a description in a *New York Times* piece that also appeared in *New Straits Times.com*, their initial meeting was described in breathless, tabloid terms.

Trump would relive those moments when he first set eyes on Melania in a 2005 *CNN* interview with talk show host Larry King. "I went crazy [when I saw her]," he recalled. "I was actually supposed to be meeting somebody else. There was this great supermodel that I was supposed to be meeting and she was sitting right next to Melania. The person that was sort of setting the meeting up said, 'Look! There's so and so!' I said 'forget about her. Who is the one on the left?'"

Their attraction was immediate and mutual. They talked easily throughout the evening. The fact that Melania was more than 20 years Trump's junior did not seem to enter into the equation. "It was great chemistry and energy. We started to talk. We had a great time. Something was 'there' right away."

By the end of the evening, there were sparks. Not surprisingly, Trump made the first move and asked for her telephone number. But Melania was playing hard to get. "I am not a girl who will just give away a number to anybody," she told *The New York Times*. But she was a woman who knew what she wanted and, three days later, she called Trump up and asked him out.

The Trump/Melania relationship developed quite naturally and quickly through 1999. People in their respective circles knew what was going on, but it would remain for a joint appearance on *The Howard Stern Show* for a public reveal of what, by that time, had evolved into a full blown relationship. By that time, Trump was totally smitten, willing to tell anyone who would ask that they were totally compatible and that they never fought.

Melania, in an *Entertainment Tonight* interview, was equally effusive in her love for The Donald. "He's a romantic guy. It's a different romance then, maybe, some other people have. But he's a very different man. We have a great relationship and we are both very independent."

And typical of all of Trump's previous relationships, they both had their separate careers and lives and would spend a lot of time apart. Which, according to *About Relationships.com*, resulted in the couple breaking up for a brief time in 1999. But they almost immediately reconciled and Melania was at his side…

When Trump announced that he was running for President.

It was not the first time Trump had considered politics as a career option. He had long been mingling with politicians as part of his day job as real estate tycoon and had an idea of how the political system worked. Trump as a Presidential candidate had been a hot topic, albeit more in idle speculation than reality, in 1988. Trump, when asked, would sidestep the possibility but, like every response to any question, Trump had left the option open for some future time. As it would turn out, Trump's political potential was being taken very seriously that same year. As revealed in the authorized book *Destiny and Power: The American Odyssey of George Herbert Walker Bush*, Trump was approached at one point as a possible running mate for Republican presidential candidate George H.W. Bush. There were many who, looking back on the situation, claimed that it was Trump who actually approached the Republican Party with the idea.

Years later, Trump would explore the former theory in a *Meet the Press* interview in which he gave then Bush aid Lee Atwater all the credit for the overture. "I was building my empire. I guess I was in the midst of it and Lee said, 'You'd be great. You should do it. I want to get back to you on this.' We talked about it on two occasions but nothing ever came of it."

More political temptation came in October 1999 when Trump was asked to throw his hat into the presidential ring as a potential representative of the upstart and considered by many fringe Reform Party. The Reform Party, which boasted such extreme right wing stars as Jesse Ventura, Ron Paul and, most recently, Republican renegade Pat Buchannan, felt that Trump, with his real world successes in business and finance, would add some real world luster to the popular notion that The Reform Party was made up of outsiders, extremists and malcontents. But, most importantly, Reform Party higher-ups got Trump's attention by appealing to his massive ego.

"It's not so much about The Reform Party," Trump explained on news show *Hardball with Chris Mathews*. "It's really the fact that I'd want to make it and that if I ran and spent a lot of money, I could actually win. I could beat the Democratic/Republican apparatus."

He further pontificated on the news show *Meet the Press* that his experience as both a casino and a real estate developer were the ideal skills needed to run the country. "I understand this stuff. I understand good times and I understand bad times. I mean, why is a politician going to do a better job than I can?"

Before officially announcing his candidacy, whose first serious attempt was chronicled by the likes of *Ballot Access News.com* and *CNN/All Politics.com*, Trump met with Reform Party officials to assess the reality of his running. Pat Buchannan was considered the early frontrunner but Trump's chances as a viable alternative were considerable. Trump filed the necessary papers and began prepping himself for what would be his first true test of his political prowess, the upcoming Reform Party California primary.

Trump received 15, 311 votes, admittedly a miniscule number but, by third party standards, the results were encouraging. A follow up primary in Michigan resulted in Trump netting an equally respectable 2,120 votes. But Trump, in the wake of these triumphs, immediately began to bristle at being part of a political movement that constantly appeared fragmented, disorganized and in a state of chaos. Trump liked the idea of playing at politics but only if the game was played by his rules. And so on February 14, 2000 Trump threw in the towel and withdrew his candidacy.

Not that the billionaire was too disappointed or bored. By 2000, Trump had seen a sudden resurgence, as witnessed by his development profile, which was going a long way toward, quite literally, making New York City his own. 2001 alone saw Trump complete construction on a massive project christened Trump World Tower, begin construction of Trump Place and begin development on Trump International Hotel and Tower; all within the confines of New York City's most upscale neighborhoods. Trump's ability to brand reached a new level as the name Trump increased the value of numerous projects on the national and international stage.

Trump's relationship with Melania continued. They were seen out and about everywhere, arm in arm and quite obviously in love. Although Melania would take some tabloid heat as Trump's beautiful but not too bright trophy wife, those who met her came away impressed with her intelligence and her ability to hold her own in conversations many cynical reporters had initially deemed well beyond her intellectual pay grade. Even those who had been quick to dismiss Trump as a buffoon, had to admit that the third time had been the charm.

Trump's ability to act like…well, Trump had long made him a target of caricature in the media and, on occasion, Hollywood would come to the mogul with the opportunity to play, essentially himself, in largely uncredited cameos in movies and television. Trump would prove his ham acting mettle in the 80's,

90's and early 2000's in the television shows *The Jeffersons*, *The Nanny*, *Spin City* and *Monk* and in the films *Home Alone 2: Lost In New York*, *The Little Rascals* and *Zoolander*.

Trump never took any of it seriously, but his acting bits did showcase a bigger than life character who was nothing if not comfortable in the glare of the spotlight. It only seemed a matter of time before Trump would break into television in a show that would very much mirror the reality of his own life.

The offer finally came in 2003 with the opportunity to host *The Apprentice*.

Successful reality show producer Mark Burnett of *Survivor* fame had an idea for a reality show which he proclaimed would be "the ultimate job interview." The premise of *The Apprentice* was immediately enticing. A group of young business and entrepreneurial-minded men and women would be put through a season-long series of job tests. At the end of each test, the person deemed the poorest performer would be 'fired. At the end of the final episode, a winner would be crowned and rewarded with a $250,000 offer sheet and a year-long apprenticeship at a top of the line business organization. Burnett did not have to look far for a template for the show. *The Apprentice* fit Trump to a T.

Which is why it took little coaxing to get the billionaire to, figuratively, take a pay cut ($50,000 an episode for the first season) to executive produce and appear as the host and arbiter of the contestants' fates. Adding further Trump to the mix was the fact that the winner would serve his or her apprenticeship at one of Trump's organizations.

But some of the very things that inspired *The Apprentice* would continue to haunt the often reckless way that Trump seemingly did business. By 2004, another of Trump's development monoliths, The Trump Hotel and Casino Resorts, filed for what would be Trump's third bankruptcy, yet another restructuring to sooth bondholders who, once again, were dealing with shaky debt. Under the terms of this latest settlement, Trump's ownership of the Trump Hotel and Casino Resorts was reduced to 27% while retaining the titles of Chairman and CEO. On the surface, it appeared as yet another black eye, but Trump managed to put a positive spin on the situation in an *Associated Press* story. "I don't think it's [the bankruptcy] is a failure. It was a success. It was really just something that worked better than other alternatives. It's really just a technical thing but it came together."

The Apprentice would premiere on NBC early in 2004 and from the onset, Trump, his ego, bloated pomposity and, yes, an admitted knowledge of just how the business world worked, morphed into the main reason to tune in. To the surprise of absolutely nobody, *The Apprentice* was an immediate hit, riding Trump, everything audiences loved and hated about him, to yet another success. And Trump took immediate steps to further cash in. NBC wanted *The Apprentice* for the long haul and they were going to have to pay for his presence. Trump wanted a raise and he got it; the $50,000 per episode would suddenly become $300,000 per episode from Season Two on.

By his own estimation, Trump had already risen to the level of 'all everything' in his world. Real estate development, books, a never-ending world of branding. Even his failures and recoveries were considered something special. But in a conversation with veteran *CNN* talk show host Larry King, even Trump had to admit that *The Apprentice* had taken him to a different level. "I thought I was well-known before but this [*The Apprentice*] is a whole different level. It's definitely bigger when you have 20 million people watching you every week."

Trump used the success *of The Apprentice* as a sign that things in his professional world could not be better. Now he felt it was time to take the next step in his personal life. On April 26, 2004, Trump and Melania became engaged. Needless to say, the always cynical media had a field day with the announcement, recalling the up and down courtship with Marla which was still a distinct memory. Good-natured speculation about when and how the engagement would dissolve into separation was tabloid fodder for weeks on end.

But this time, things would be different. Trump was serious about Melania in a way, truth be known, he had not been with wives one and two. Trump was in a state of bliss and ease with the prospect of finally settling down for good. He would address that very topic in October 2004 with a quote archived by *Donald Trump Quotes IMDB.com.*

"If you have to work at a marriage, it's not going to work. It [marriage] has to be sort of a natural thing. Melania makes my life easy. One of the things I so love about her is that she makes my life easier. I've never had anybody who has made my life so easy."

Some years later, Melania would, likewise, address life with her dream man in a *People* conversation. "He is who he is. Even if you give him advice, he will maybe take it but then he will do it the way he wants to do it. You cannot change a person."

When Trump popped the question, he recalled that it was all quite natural and almost an after-thought as he explained in a conversation with Larry King. "We were together five years. We were very comfortable and we got along. And one day I just said ,'You know what? It's time.'"

It would be a relatively short engagement, as the couple would soon announce their wedding day would be on January 2, 2005. Trump had never been so decisive when it came to relationships and matrimony, and he told *People* as much shortly before the wedding when he said, "If I didn't have a great woman, I would be much more nervous. I think it [the marriage] will be very successful."

The consensus was that Trump's third wedding would be lavish, big and bombastic. But Trump was not about to turn his third trip down the aisle into a three-ring circus. When it was suggested in some corners that a deal might be made to televise the wedding, Trump put his foot down and said no. But that did not mean the ceremony would be quiet and small.

Held in a church in Palm Beach, Florida, the marriage of Trump and Melania (*tres elgante* in a $200,000 wedding gown) was, as reported by such outlets as *People* and the *Palm Beach Post*, attended by more than 500 guests that included Oprah Winfrey, Clint Eastwood, Elton John, Prince Charles of England, Prince Albert of Monaco, David Letterman, then-Governor Arnold Schwarzenegger, and the

Clintons. Also on the guest list was superstar singer-songwriter Billy Joel who got behind the microphone during the after-party and celebrated the newlyweds with a rendition of "Just The Way You Are."

It was not long after saying their 'I do's' that Trump and Melania were already making plans for the future. According to a conversation with *People* following the wedding, Trump, still somewhat giddy at the notion that, at age 58, he had found a love that he felt would last, was talking about expanding his family. "Melania would like to have children. And I'm up for it."

Chapter Twelve
Hints and Teases

As it turned out, Trump was definitely up for it as, only a few short months after the marriage, Melania was pregnant.

The couple was elated and, by all accounts, Trump was attentive during the months leading up to the birth of Barron William Trump on March 20, 2006. But attentive in Trump's world also meant that he was away a lot on business. Melania knew what she was getting into when she married Trump and so was not surprised when he was in and out of town on a regular basis during her pregnancy.

As always, Trump was driven to find the next deal and the next one after that. And there were plenty of investors and developers who, despite his series of bankruptcies and the cutting of corners that marked his career path, were willing to deal with him. *The Apprentice* had him riding high. His never-ending inspirational, instructional and biographical books all did well and even some of his more flighty, but to varying degrees profitable experiments, such as Trump Model Management, Trump Shuttle, Trump Mortgage, Trump Vodka, Trump Steaks and a temporary side gig lecturing would be Trumps in a series of Real Estate Wealth Expos at a fee of $1.5 million per appearance.

But despite success upon success, Trump could occasionally wax humble in the face of it all as he offered in an interview with *CNN's* Larry King. "First of all, I'm a real estate guy. That's what I love. To give that up would be sort of like giving up my day job. I'm doing a lot of things but, always for me, it's real estate."

And into 2005-2006 he was seeing a resurgence, by Trump standards, in his real estate prospects. He had recently completed the development of a nine-story building in Chicago and a world-class golf course in Los Angeles. It was a given that a lot of people did not like Trump, personally or professionally and would often say as much (although usually behind his back or off the record) but these same people were quick to work with him because, in the world in which they traveled, they knew that Trump meant money.

But when not closing a deal or playing hardball in a meeting or dealing with the long hours it took to film an episode of *The Apprentice*, he was also finding time to be at home with his newborn and, in a conversation with *The Real Deal.com,* he was that rarity—humble and philosophical Trump, on what it was like to be a father late in life. "I think I appreciate it a little bit more. I think when you're getting older and you have a young baby, it makes you appreciate all of them [his children] more."

Trump has often, backhandedly, boasted that while he has never been the ideal husband, nobody could argue with the way he's raised his four eldest children who had, by the time Trump had child number five, gone on to have successful personal and professional lives. Trump, who had often acknowledged that he inherited his parenting skills from his parents and, especially his father, gave *The View* an abbreviated version of the Trump approach to parenting. "I kiss them. I love them. I hug them. And then after four minutes, I go back to my phone call. I'm not really a father who will go to the park and play catch."

But by the mid 2000's, he was also a bigger than life figure who could, apparently, not shake the specter of politics and his potential place in them. In 2004, it was once again floated that Trump was considering throwing his hat into the presidential ring. But it was something that Trump, owing to his increased workload, dismissed the suggestion with "I'm mulling it over" (*CNN*).

However, given Trump's reputation for dancing around any suggestion, nobody acknowledged that the thought had not crossed Trump's mind and that this dismissal might, in fact, be the first in a long series of denials, hints and teases that were masking the fact that Trump was, seriously "mulling it over."

The political bug would come around two years later, in 2006, when unhappiness with the current New York Governor, Andrew Cuomo, led to a fringe element of the Republican Party lobbying Trump about the possibility of running against Cuomo. His response to the rumor, as reported in the likes of *The New York Post*, *Mashable.com* and the television show *Fox and Friends*, seemed to pretty much mirror his dance from 2004. He went from "seriously considering it" to "It would be really interesting but I haven't really thought about it." to teasing that "I might just run as an independent in 2008."

Seemingly like clockwork, 2008 came around and suddenly Trump's name was once again in the political crosshairs, this time being actively rumored as the Republican's best bet to go up against Barack Obama. Trump trotted out his previous 'I'm thinking of running' comments before ultimately doing an opinion 180 and being very complimentary toward Obama before finally throwing his support behind Republican candidate John McCain.

Political pundits were kept on their toes. When it came to politics, Trump was a chameleon; changing his attitude toward politics in an arbitrary manner, betraying, by degrees, his Republican roots and being free and easy in who he supported. And at the end of the day, he was always 'thinking' about running for office. Going into 2009, the question was constantly in the air. Would he or wouldn't he?

Chapter Thirteen
Who Do You Think You Are?

The Apprentice would turn out to be more than a long running reality show hosted by a bombastic real life caricature. Truth be told, *The Apprentice* was something special. It was Trump's entry into a real world populated by real people.

Granted, Trump had long been the undeclared spearhead of a thriving, energetic and truly hardcore plateau of economic and real estate dominance. The type of game Trump played was now, often front-page news rather than buried in the business or real estate pages. There were glowing profiles and headlines trumpeting the latest important deal and the stop-the-presses, blockbuster development. Trump, to a very large sense was a rock star. But he was, for all intents and purposes, a rock star playing to a very limited audience.

Because Trump was around 'his type of people,' those in the business, those who traveled in the same sequestered circles and, most importantly, those who did not live paycheck to paycheck. Trump was around royalty but he was not around real people.

The Apprentice would finally give him the

opportunity to be, vicariously, invited into working-class living rooms where, on a weekly basis, he could instruct the people, who worked hard for their money, how the upper class played the game.

From the outset, Trump was in hog heaven playing himself in a slightly sanitized television world. Trump would be the first to acknowledge that *The Apprentice* was hard work, long hours and a facsimile of how his world really worked. Trump loved playing the comic book ogre, weekly stomping on dreams and holding the financial death sentence of "you're fired" over contestants' heads. With Trump as the ringmaster, one could not help but learn something about how Trump's version of the real world worked.

What it would ultimately become was high camp, faux drama and highly forced and choreographed conflict. And Trump was like a little kid amidst it all. When his dismissive catch phrase "you're fired" unexpectedly struck a nerve in pop culture circles, he promptly copyrighted the phrase for trademark purposes.

He was quick to also take advantage of the show to turn a buck in every way. After the first season, Trump negotiated a hefty per episode raise. As the season's progressed, he negotiated his way to an executive producer challenge which would, ultimately, help when its success spawned more than two dozen licensed versions of the show internationally. Trump was not above product placement and episodes of *The Apprentice* would regularly feature his products and brands. Occasionally *The Apprentice* would become a family affair as Trump's sons Donald Trump Jr. and Eric Trump and daughter Ivanka, would appear on the show as judges and even wife Melania would take a turn in front of the camera when she had something to promote.

During Trump's tour of duty on *The Apprentice*, there were some controversies and, yes, bad blood. According to a *Newsweek* piece, each season's winner was to receive the title of "Executive Vice President" and work as an 'owner's representative' on a Trump or other related property. The reality was that their title was nothing more than a publicity spokesperson who earned their pay appearing at events to help promote sales of Trump Organization properties.

The Apprentice: Martha Stewart seemed like a natural at the development stage. Replace Trump with a female billionaire. Simple as that. But simple did not translate into success and the show, was canceled after one season, amid charges by Stewart that Trump had sabotaged the show. Trump denied all charges and he and Stewart have not spoken since.

For Trump, *The Apprentice* presented seemingly countless spin-off opportunities. *Celebrity Apprentice* would put B list and under celebrities to the Trump challenge. Trump also took an executive producer role in the Trump-style dating game entitled *Donald Trump Presents The Ultimate Merger* in which one of the most controversial *Apprentice* candidates, Omarosa Manigault, would whittle down a list of romantic suitors picked by Trump.

Trump's stay on *The Apprentice* would be a long and lucrative one. In fact, Trump would still, most likely, be on the show now if his presidential ambitions had not gotten in the way. There was some debate as to whether the show would survive without him. NBC decided it could and, recently, named Arnold Schwarzenegger as Trump's replacement. *The Apprentice* would go on. But one thing was certain: It would not be the same.

Chapter Fourteen
My Lawyer's Bigger Than Your Lawyer

While Trump's business interests thrived in the later part of the 2000's, his legal bills were also going through the roof.

Trump had a long history of suing or being sued at the drop of a hat. He was often in court on everything from legitimate legal and business challenges to reasons that seemed marginal and borderline frivolous at best. And at other times, it seemed to the public that going to court was a public relations ploy, designed to keep his name in the papers or to prove a point to his satisfaction.

"Trump has been the target of hundreds of civil lawsuits or has initiated lawsuits," said attorney Alan Gartner, one of a group of lawyers Trump kept busy, in a *YahooPolitics.com* story. "It's a natural part of doing business in this country."

Typical of the lengths Trump would go to to make a point occurred in 1990 when, as reported by *The New York Times* and *Philly.com*, the billionaire brought a suit against the brokerage agency, Janney Montgomery Scott and, particularly, its employee Marvin Roffman on the grounds that Roffman, during an interview with *The Wall Street Journal*, had said that Trump's Taj Mahal project would initially break records but fail by the end of the year. Trump and his legal team demanded that the brokerage firm either publically recant Roffman's statements or that Roffman be fired. The firm blinked and Roffman was fired. Long story short, Trump declared bankruptcy on the Taj Mahal in November 1990 and Roffman countersued for defamation of character and loss of employment to the tune of $2 million, largely on the research that indicated Roffman's statements had been accurate. That suit was settled out of court and Trump would not have any comment.

It had long been speculated in economic circles that Trump allegedly might be occasionally cooking the books (releasing false financial information), a common occurrence in the shadowy world of high finance. As reported by *Sec.gov.com*, the Securities and Exchange Commission had their suspicions in 2002 and brought a suit against Trump Hotels and Casinos on the grounds that the organization had released misleading financial figures in a 1999 earnings release. This case was quickly settled but on a dubious note in which Trump did not have to either admit or deny the charges.

Trump had a hair trigger temper when it came to the media. Trump had a preconceived notion of how he wanted himself presented to the world and so, in 2006, he was immediately on the horn to his lawyers when he felt his financial net worth was misrepresented in author Timothy O'Brien's book *Trump Nation*. O'Brien, through three different sources, and as reported by *The Atlantic*, stated that Trump was worth $150-$250 million, on the low side when compared to Trump's estimation of $4-$6 billion. In filing the $5 billion lawsuit against the author and his publisher, Trump claimed that the author's low estimate had hurt his reputation and had cost him specific business deals. The suit was dismissed in July 2009 and a follow up appeal failed in 2011. Trump would lick his wounds when he groused to *The Atlantic's* William D. Cohan, "Essentially the judge said Trump is too famous. He's so famous that you're allowed to say anything you want about him. Well I disagree with that."

The majority of Trump's calls for legal action during the late 2000's tended to fall on the side of, by degrees, serious business; a feud with Deutsche Bank for what he deemed 'predatory loan practices' when he asked for a loan extension and the opportunity to lower prices on slow moving units in a Chicago hotel and condominium complex. Inevitably suits flew in both directions, the case dragged out for years and, as in many cases of this kind, was dismissed. But there were those occasional cases in which frivolous and downright silly was the order of the day. A loser in a Miss Universe pageant sued Trump on the grounds that it was fixed to favor certain contestants and was literally laughed out of court.

And then there was the night in 2013 that left-leaning comedian Bill Maher appeared on *The Tonight Show* and, as reported by many media outlets including *The Atlantic*, offered Trump $5 million if he could offer proof that his father was not an Orangutan. Said in obvious jest and in response to Trump's offer of $5 million to President Obama for copies of his college and passport applications (in his ongoing crusade to prove Obama was not a US citizen). Trump responded to the challenge by sending Maher a copy of his birth certificate and hinted at legal action if a check from Maher was not forthcoming.

Maher did not immediately respond and Trump

told *The Atlantic* that "he has not responded and the reason he has not responded is that his lawyers have probably told him 'You've got yourself a problem.'"

Maher finally did respond and, as reported in *The Atlantic*, said "Donald Trump must learn two things, what a joke is and what a contract is."

Trump's mania for what he perceived as 'branding' reached new highs of inanity in the 1980's when, in a case chronicled by *The New York Times* he sent his lawyer around to a company called Trump Group and advised its owners, Jules and Eddie Trump, who also, coincidentally, happened to be real estate developers in their own right, that they could no longer use the last names they were born with.

Jules and Eddie, who had been on this earth longer than Trump had, were, needless to say, amused and then shocked. According to Trump's lawyer, there had been confusion in the business community on several occasions between Trump and his Trump Organization and Jules and Eddie's Trump Group and that the brother's use of their given name in a business setting had been designed to reap the benefits of Donald Trump's work and accomplishments and that their use of their own name constituted unfair competition.

Trump was insistent that he was in the right and, after a lot of litigation, the case was ultimately brought to the New York State Supreme Court where Trump lost. But Trump held no animosity against the Trump brothers as he explained to *The New York Times*. "They're really nice guys. They're quality guys. They do quality developments. I'm friends with them. I never sue people who I know and like.

"I just didn't know them then."

Chapter Fifteen
Politics as Unusual

In December 2011, Trump cracked the top six most admired men and women in a *USA Today/Gallup Poll*. But when it came to his political philosophy and where his party loyalty stood, he was still very much a man of mystery.

In a piece conducted by *Politifact.com*, Trump, since 1987, had been a Republican, a Reform Party member, a Democrat, a Republican, an Independent and a Republican again. He was also on record in the piece as having contributed to both Democratic and Republican campaigns. Politically he seemed to lean heavily conservative in Republican hot button issues. He was pro-life, anti-gun control and in line with the party on all manner of military and economic issues. He would occasionally waffle on the subject of gay rights and seemed dead set against most forms of immigration, illegal or otherwise. But for those in the far right of conservative politics, who going into 2011 were once again eyeing Trump as potential Presidential timber, nobody was truly sure where Trump stood. Even Trump.

"I was from an area [Manhattan] that was pretty much all Democrat," Trump said in a *Face The Nation* television interview. "And frankly over the years, as I have gotten more and more involved, I have evolved."

In fact, Trump was so evasive when it came to politics that, possibly more on a whim than anything else, he confused political observers even further when, in December 2011, while still a Republican, he checked 'I do not wish to enroll in a party,' on his registration form. Trump attorney Michael Cohen told *Politico.com* that Trump made that decision "in order to preserve his right to run as an independent candidate if he is not pleased with the eventual GOP nominee."

Truth be told, Trump was giving serious consideration to actually running because he felt that those Republicans already in the race, including the likes of Mitt Romney and Mike Huckabee, would not stand a chance against the incumbent Obama who, well ahead of the nominating convention was already polling at 50% nationally, and Trump felt he had the polls to back up his thinking.

A February 2011 *Newsweek* poll showed Trump within a few points of Obama in head to head competition while an April *Public Policy Poll* gave Trump a nine-point lead among all contenders for the Republican nomination.

In the meantime Trump, who seemingly never found a reporter or television talk show host he didn't like, was in high demand and making the rounds, acting coy and seemingly above it all, yet making it abundantly clear that he was not only considering a run for The White House but was serious about it. In a conversation with *Fox News*, Trump said, "A lot of people in the polls don't vote for me because they think I'm just having a good time. I am absolutely not."

It was in April that Trump showed just how serious he was when he planted the seeds of speculation that Obama might not have been born in the US and, as such, would not be eligible to be the President of The United States. Alternately coy yet insistent, Trump was quite good at spreading the seeds of suspicion and innuendo. Needless to say the press, who were seemingly denigrating their profession with the frantic pursuit of headlines from even the most questionable sources, were lining up to take in Trump's non-candidacy and his conspiracy theory.

Throughout April, Trump was everywhere, allegedly to promote his latest television spinoff, *Celebrity Apprentice*, but his ulterior motive regarding Obama was almost immediately the talking point that everybody from *CNN, The Washington Post, NBC News* and countless other media outlets were lining up to spread the gospel of unsubstantiated reports from the mouth of Trump.

And Trump was perfect in his sincerity.

"Three weeks ago, when I started, I thought he was probably born in this country," Trump told *The Today Show*. "Right now I have some real doubts."

Trump continued to stir the controversy when, in mid -April, he claimed that he had dispatched several private detectives to Hawaii, Obama's birth place, to search out the truth behind the recently coined 'birther movement' that now had Trump as the center stage ringmaster. Although ultimately the detectives found nothing to substantiate Trump's claims, he continued to proclaim that his team of hired private detectives was on the verge of a major discovery. He breathlessly told *NBC News* that, "My investigators might uncover one of the greatest cons in the history of politics and beyond."

Along the way, the inevitable side note to the Obama controversy was that Trump still had not made up his mind whether he would enter the Presidential race in 2012. But it soon became evident that Trump had become the master manipulator of thoughts, minds and the media. By the end of April, Trump's insistence on questioning Obama's place of birth had grown into a rallying cry so potent and adamant that Obama's hand was forced and he was compelled to produce a very legal birth certificate that dampened the controversy.

But during a meeting with reporters shortly after the release of Obama's birth certificate, Trump told *CBS News* and other media "I am really honored, frankly, to have played such a big role in, hopefully, getting rid of this issue. We have to look at it [the birth certificate]. We have to see is it real, is it proper, what's on it? But I hope it checks out."

In that same press conference, Trump was eye rolling and tongue in cheek when, talking about the importance of the presidency. he emphatically said "We are not going to be able to solve our problems if we are distracted by side shows and carnival barkers."

Whatever agenda Trump had in stirring things up had, at least to his way of thinking, run its course, as had his apparent interest in winning the top job in the land. On May 16, 2011 in an official statement to the press that included *CNN*, Trump said thanks but no thanks to a serious presidential run.

"After considerable deliberation and reflection, I have decided not to pursue the office of the presidency," the statement read in part. "Ultimately business is my greatest passion and I am not ready to leave the private sector. I will not be running for President as much as I would like to."

Eventually, Trump would throw his support behind the Republican nominee, Mitt Romney. But within a week of saying he would not run in 2012, Trump was making a lot of noise in the direction of 2016.*The New York Post* and other outlets reported that Trump had spent $1 million on state-by-state electoral research to help determine how viable a Presidential candidate he would be.

Michael Cohen, executive vice president and special counsel to Trump, confirmed the research to *The New York Post*. "The electoral research was commissioned. We did not spend $1 million on this research for it to just sit on my bookshelf. At this point, Mr. Trump has not made any decision on a political run."

But Trump, in the wake of his 2012 withdrawal from the race, was more than willing to entertain the possibility during press interviews and speaking engagements through the next couple of years. At a speech in Michigan, as reported by *The New York Post*, Trump responded to the question of if and when he would take the big political plunge by saying, "Everybody tells me 'please run for President.' I would be much happier if a great and competent person came along. I would love to see somebody come in who is going to be great."

Trump was doing more than merely entertaining speculation. More and more Trump's voice was heard in discussions of the many important political and social issues of the day. He was an early and vocal supporter of a popular government backed bailout plan for the auto industry, one that immediately put Trump in the good graces of the traditionally pivotal election year state of Michigan. Trying to appeal to all levels of the populace would, occasionally, cause Trump's opinions and logic to come across as skewed toward illogic and fringe thoughts. He would stub his toes on the controversial question of school age children being vaccinated when he speculated that vaccinations against childhood diseases could cause Autism, a claim he repeated during the Republican primary debate on September 16, 2015, long debunked by the Center for Disease Control, the American Academy of Pediatrics, and the World Health Organization. He also ran afoul of the scientific community when he weighed in on the question of global warming by stating that the fact that the world has winter proves that there is no global warming in a post on Twitter in October, 2015. "It's really cold outside, they are calling it a major freeze, weeks ahead of normal. Man, we could use a big fat dose of global warming!"

What many expected would be Trump's official coming out as a viable political candidate came off as more of a stumbling start when Trump spoke at the Conservative Political Action Conference, a gathering of right-oriented political power brokers. Trump's speech was scheduled for 8:30 a.m., early for most convention goers, and the result was that Trump ended up speaking before a half empty ballroom. But for those who did show up, they were given a preview of how Trump would react when he was officially out on the presidential stump. His speech was long and meandering and, as reported by *Yahoo News.com*, one attendee complained that Trump's talk was filled to overflowing with 'I' and 'Me.' During this speech, Trump would elicit the strongest response from the sparse audience when he said that if he were president, he would take Iraq's oil and use the proceeds to pay $1 million to each family of an American soldier who died in the war.

But even those controversial statements served their purpose. They got him in the headlines and, for better or worse, a number of potential voters who, at this stage lived and died by everything he said, believed him. Trump's bravado, outrageousness and ego-driven persona was considered contrary to the tried and true Republican way of doing things, but with the GOP largely moribund and, to the public at large, out of touch with the reality of working people, Trump, in many quarters, continued to present the cure to what ailed them.

Easily the first serious consideration for Trump came in October of 2013 when a group of New York based Republican big wigs began circulating a state-wide memo, strongly suggesting that Trump run for governor against the current governor, Democrat Andrew Cuomo. Trump would claim that he was oblivious to the offer, reported by *USA Today* from an interview on the television show *Fox and Friends*. He played humble Trump on the offer. "I haven't even thought about it. It would be very interesting but it's not something that is of great interest to me."

The reason being that Trump, at the urging of important Republicans and the favorable results of his research on his state wide prospects, was, by 2014, already laying the groundwork for a legitimate run at the White House. So were a number of other candidates.

Going into the 2016 Presidential race, the Republicans were feeling their oats. They were coming off a mid-term congressional election in which they took over the Senate and took a big bite out of the Democrats' hold on the House of Representatives. Obama had just officially entered 'lame duck status' in his final year of office and the probable Democratic successor was shaping up to be Hillary Clinton, who the Republicans felt was vulnerable.

Consequently when it came time to officially throw hats into the ring, a very long list of Republicans did. The top tier included established as well as fringe candidates including former Florida Governor Jeb Bush, retired neurosurgeon Ben Carson, New Jersey Governor Chris Christie, Texas Senator Ted Cruz, former Hewlitt-Packard CEO Carly Fiorina, Ohio Governor John Kasich, Kentucky Senator Rand Paul, and Florida Senator Marco Rubio. Trump felt he would be quite comfortable and unbeatable in this mix.

His first step, and a risky one at that, involved not renewing his contract with NBC for the shows *The Apprentice* and *Celebrity Apprentice*. Risky in that Trump would be walking away from a lot of money and, given his nature, that was not something he would ever be likely to do. "NBC wants me to renew it," Trump told *The New Hampshire Union Leader*. "I told them I'm not ready. I'm seriously considering running [for President] right now."

Trump was also meeting and gathering a team of veteran Republican operatives who, he boasted, would make up a solid core of advisors should he actually decide to run. He also acknowledged in *The New Hampshire Union Leader* that, should he decide to run, he would not accept campaign donations or contributions and that his entire campaign would be self-funded. "The company has a strong cash flow," he said. "We would provide the funding ourselves."

Observers who had thought of Trump entering the political arena as a long running joke, were now beginning to take Trump a bit more seriously. The other shoe would drop in February 2015, when *The New Hampshire Union Leader* interviewed Trump and came away with journalistic gold. "I am seriously considering a run for President of the United States in 2016. We are forming an exploratory committee in New Hampshire. We could be ready to officially announce that in April.

"I would expect to make a final decision on whether or not I will run by early June."

Chapter Sixteen
Enter the Donald

It was not what people expected. Or maybe it was. On June 16, 2015, Trump made the grandest of entrances down an escalator from the upper levels of Trump Tower. Cameras flashed. The crowd applauded frantically. It was like a medieval procession. Trump was king, smiling broadly and waving to his followers, his minions, as Neil Young's "Rockin' In The Free World" echoed and reverberated through the concrete and steel.

Trump was about to declare his candidacy for the Republican nomination for President of the United States. And he was going to do it his way.

After a spirited introduction from his daughter Ivanka, Trump took to the microphone amid thunderous applause. What followed would be the ultimate political E Ticket ride, a record 45 minutes and change full of fire, self-aggrandizement, insult and bombast. There were not a lot of specifics on how he would solve the country's problems, but a whole lot of exposition on what the problems were, in his opinion, and what he would do about them were the part and parcel of a speech that was literally all over the place.

Trump's boasts that "I don't need money from donors. I have my own money. I'm really rich," almost immediately brought down the house. He was equally effusive in trotting out what would become catch phrases such as "I pledge to restore the American dream" and "I will be the greatest jobs President that God ever created." But as the speech went on, Trump threw figurative red meat to a hungry crowd when he addressed the hot button issue of illegal immigration.

"When Mexico sends its people, they're not sending their best. They're sending people who have lots of problems. They're bringing drugs. They're bringing crime. They're rapists. And some, I assume, are good people."

Trump's answer to stemming the tide of illegal immigration on that day was typical Trump. "I would build a great wall and nobody builds walls better than me. I will build a great wall on our southern border and I'll have Mexico pay for that wall."

Over the course of his announcement, Trump literally threw out every problem the country had and the inequities that had been allowed to fester and grow between the US and foreign countries. On the importance of having a strong military at a time of encroaching terrorism, Trump exclaimed, "Our enemies are getting stronger and our country is getting weaker. I love the military and I want to have the strongest military we've ever had. I will keep Iran from acquiring nuclear weapons." When it came to what he perceived as high unemployment in America, he offered up, "A lot of people can't get jobs because there are no jobs because China has our jobs and Mexico has our jobs. I'll bring back jobs from China,

Mexico and Japan. I'll bring back our jobs and I'll bring back our money."

And as for Obamacare, the controversial medical insurance program implemented by The White House, Trump was dismissive when he said, "It's virtually worthless. It's a disaster."

Shortly after ending his announcement, the Trump campaign was literally off and running. Trump flew to Iowa and, shortly thereafter, New Hampshire, the first two scheduled primaries, to begin campaigning in earnest. In his wake, he left havoc, confusion, controversy and a decidedly mixed reaction from the press. Critiques ranged from negative to mixed to positive. Most outlets picked up on the circus atmosphere of it all but, for the time being, seemed inclined to give Trump the benefit of the doubt. *Politico.com* caught the tenor of the occasion when it assessed that Trump's announcement was "discursive, pugnacious, bizarre and most entertaining."

The first shot back came from Neil Young who made it clear that he was supporting Bernie Sanders, and strongly suggested that Trump not use his song at his campaign events.

A second shot was not far behind when it was reported in such outlets as *The Hollywood Reporter*, *The Huffington Post* and *Business Insider* that the Trump campaign had paid extras $50 each to come to his rally and cheer. A leaked memo was traced to the *Extra Mile Casting Agency* and *Gotham Government Relations and Communications* (a political consulting group that had worked with Trump in the past). Both agencies either refused comment or denied, as did the Trump campaign leadership.

Not surprisingly, Trump's inflammatory and, to many, racist remarks regarding illegal immigrants, and Mexicans in particular, brought an angry and immediate backlash from Mexican-Americans (who cringing Republicans had been counting on as support in their hope for return to The White House) and corporate America. Immediately cutting off all ties (including lucrative business arrangements) with the Trump Organization were NBC, Macy's, Univision and NASCAR. Trump's remarks provided an immediate media firestorm with outlets including CBS News, Fox News, The Washington Post, CNN, the Associated Press and countless others.

Trump seemed surprised that his one remark had caused such an immediate public relations nightmare. It was not a surprise that he bobbed and weaved during an interview with *Fox News* but, ultimately, refused to back down.

"I didn't know it was going to be quite this severe," he said. "But I really knew it was going to be bad. It seems like I'm sort of the whipping post because I bring it up."

Chapter Seventeen
When Republicans Collide

Unfortunately for the other candidates for the Republican nomination, Trump's 'anti-immigrant' remarks were figuratively tarring them with the same brush. Rather than pushing their own campaigns and agendas, the already crowded field was faced with having to answer Trump's comments. For those candidates, it immediately evolved into a lose-lose situation. Agree with Trump and they would be adding immediate legitimacy to his candidacy. Disagree and they would be running the risk of being attached to an idea they had not really thought out yet. But a few, some with caution, weighed in.

Ben Carson said, "Trump's wording was, perhaps, a little inflammatory but this is more a consequence of Trump's incendiary style. Trump's core message about illegal immigration was correct."

Ted Cruz agreed with Trump in principle. "The need to address illegal immigration should no longer be ignored. Trump has a bold, brash colorful way of speaking. I do not intend to attack Trump over his specific phrasing. "

Like Trump, Marco Rubio was succinct and to the point. "Trump's comments were not just offensive and inaccurate but also divisive."

Following his announcement, Trump went to Iowa where his first actual campaign stop, as reported by The Des Moines Register, pretty much set the template for how the Trump campaign would go. From his opening remarks, it was blast furnace attacks against Republican candidates Jeb Bush and Marco Rubio. And his remarks were not just against his own party. At one point, he slammed Democrat Hillary Clinton for "playing the woman's card." During an off the cuff question and answer session, Trump acknowledged, "I'm proud to say I'm pro-life."He also took dead aim at terrorism and, particularly, ISIS when he said, "ISIS has the oil and ISIS is rich. And what we should do now is go blast the hell out of that oil."

The remark was greeted with wild cheers and applause. Trump was on his way. Next stop Manchester, New Hampshire.

It did not take long for Trump to figure out what people on the stump wanted to hear. People in New Hampshire, as reported by 7News Boston, were treated to more politician bashing, a shot against the recently freed alleged army deserter Bowe Bergdahl and uplifting rhetoric. "The American Dream is dead. But we will bring it back bigger, stronger and more powerful than ever before." Trump continued to slam Mexicans and illegal immigration. "I love Mexicans," he told the New Hampshire crowd. "I have so many Mexican friends. But the people who are coming into our country are, in many cases, brutal." The surreal nature of the moment was magnified when pro-Mexican protestors at the rally were thrown out of the building where Trump was speaking.

Trump's rush to the campaign trail was having

the desired impact in the polls. *The Boston Globe* reported that, after a mere two speeches, Trump had climbed to second place in polls in Iowa, New Hampshire and nationally. These spikes were a magnet that was suddenly drawing the media in bunches.

CNN in particular was over the moon about Trump in the early days of the campaign offering extensive, often seemingly around the clock airtime on all of their news and interview blocks. Other outlets would be even more blatant in their courtship of Trump, to the point that other campaigns had begun to complain that their candidates were being offered scraps or nothing at all.

Trump's relationship with the media during his presidential campaign has been a startling turnabout. Make no mistake, Trump has always equated success with exposure and has always been fairly easy when it came to doing interviews and offering up a pithy bon mot suitable for a headline. But over the years Trump has learned that the press will turn on him in a second; a lesson often learned during his economic ups and downs and some of the more tawdry elements of his personal life.

But it appears that a truce has been called with his entry into the Presidential race. The trade-off appears to be simple. Trump will talk to just about anybody who asks and the press in exchange gets ratings, higher ad rates and their collective reputations tarnished with endless rounds of infomercial style interviews in which no really hard, persistent or probing questions are asked and the reporters come across, for the most part, as submissive foils who sit back and allow Trump to, essentially, walk all over the verbal landscape, saying what he wants.

Even that has not completely placated Trump. In an interview with 60 Minutes around the time of his presidential announcement, Trump made it plain that his love/hate relationship with the press was, at this point, mostly hate. "I don't like lies. I don't mind a bad story. If you did a bad story on me, if it were a fair story, I wouldn't be thin-skinned at all. A pretty good percentage of the media are a terrible group of people. They write lies. They write false stories. But I can take it. I can take it if it's fair."

By the time Trump hit the first swing through the west early in July, he appeared to have his speech down to a surreal series of talking points. Unlike the other candidates who were often described as reading from pre-planned scripts with a distinct lack of passion, Trump had no script, there was no sense of order but, rather a rambling, often disjointed look at what he felt was wrong and how he would fix it, albeit, at this point in the campaign, there was nothing concrete in how things would be fixed but, more often than not, a lot of passionate sloganeering with just enough space for, admittedly, rabid followers to whoop and holler.

Los Angeles, Las Vegas and Phoenix, as reported by the *Las Vegas Sun*, were typical Trump. He would attack the other candidates, in particular, Jeb Bush and Marco Rubio who he seemed to consider his major competition, as well as Hillary Clinton and President Obama. There were moments where terrorism, the economy and jobs had their moments of vitriol. But Trump sensed what would create the most controversy, and by association headlines, and so he hammered particularly hard on illegal immigration and

Mexicans. In Los Angeles, he added to the anti-Mexican sentiment by appearing with families that had been affected by undocumented immigrant crime.

"We have to stop illegals from coming into the country," he told a cheering crowd in Los Angeles. "Mexico is smart. They're sending us their problems."

Trump stood triumphant amid the cheering thousands in Phoenix. In his mind, he could do no wrong. And that may well have created his first misstep. Shortly after the conclusion of the Phoenix speech, Arizona Senator John McCain summed up the experience by stating in an *Associated Press* story, "Trump's racist barbs had fired up the crazies." When Trump got wind of McCain's remarks, he fired back. "McCain is a dummy who graduated at the bottom of his class at the Naval Academy." Trump must have realized that he had bitten off more than he could chew. McCain had long been considered a decorated war hero whose exploits as a pilot and courage during his stay in a prisoner of war camp were well known. To attack a certified hero was sacrilege in many quarters, as Trump would find out later in July during a speech in Ames, Iowa.

Loud boos mixed with the expected cheers cascaded down on Trump. But the candidate, quite full of himself, ignored them and when asked about his disparaging remarks against McCain, blasted McCain as not being a real war hero. "He was a war hero because he was captured. I like people who were not captured."

The boos continued. Trump's shoot from the hip attitude had finally gotten him in trouble. The fallout was immediate. Some of Trump's most ardent supporters were veterans or knew people who served in the military. But Trump's comments, now coupled with stories of how he avoided military duty quickly resurfacing, were causing many to think twice. And the other Republican candidates, some of whom were veterans or pro-military, saw an opening and were quick to admonish Trump for attacking McCain. Candidates and former Governors George Pataki, of New York, and Rick Perry, of Texas, openly called for Trump to quit the race over his remarks about McCain. Others called for restraint. Ultimately Trump had the final say when, on the news show This Week, he told reporter Martha Radditz that he would not apologize to McCain for his remarks.

While many observers turned up their noses at what they considered Trump's racist and inflammatory remarks and attitudes and his three ring circus of a presentation, they had to concede that Trump's political antics were drawing a lot of attention in a Republican field that, only weeks into the campaign, was looking tired, boring and, most importantly, not likely to produce a candidate that could win back the White House for the Republicans. Many realistic naysayers predicted that Trump's show would burn out after a fairly short run.

But by July 9, two poles were released, as reported by *The Business Insider*, that Trump had, in fact, surged to the lead in both The Economist/YouGov.com and the Public Policy Polling Survey among all the current Republican candidates.

Trump could go from, by his standards, serious candidate to mean little kid in the blink of an eye. Buoyed by a sizeable, fanatic following that he claimed supported him despite his anti-McCain remarks, Trump became increasingly volatile when he perceived he was under attack and could act out in seemingly immature ways. One such incident occurred late in July when another candidate, Senator Lindsey Graham, referred to Trump as "a jackass." Trump made note of Graham's comments during a speech in Graham's home state of South Carolina before getting even in a very public manner by giving out Graham's personal telephone number for the entire world to hear. Graham was deluged with calls and subsequently would joke that it was no big deal and required nothing more than getting a new phone number. But the consensus was that Trump had won that round.

It was around this time that the first serious conspiracy surrounding Trump and the validity of his campaign was floated. Established media outlets including *The Washington Post,* Salon.com and *Esquire*, as well as obscure bloggers like Antiwar.com and Black Bag.com, began reporting, in varying degrees of detail, that Trump and Clinton were actually in cahoots on a plot dubbed 'The False Flag Conspiracy' in which Trump was allegedly running for the Republican nomination to ensure that Clinton would win the White House, based on the assumption that Trump could not beat Clinton as either a Republican or an Independent. Neither Clinton nor Trump would ever comment.

Trump's continued slams about illegal immigration continued to be the driving theme of his campaign and he felt it was time to add a bit of drama and theatrics by showing up at the US/Mexico border and mixing and mingling with border patrol agents.

Trump's private airplane touched down on July 22 where a crowd of reporters, protesters and a good number of supporters met him. Trump disembarked wearing a baseball cap that had his campaign slogan, Make America Great Again, emblazoned on it and was driven to an area just across the road from the notoriously unstable border town of Nuevo Laredo. He spoke before a crowd near a well-known border crossing, many of them not quite sure what the purpose of the visit was.

If the purpose was to attack illegal immigration, then the backdrop was ideal. But in reality what the audience received was a slight variation on Trump's regular stump speech; bashing Mexicans but also, suddenly, being a bit even handed on the subject. As covered by the Associated Press and others, Trump seemed unusually generous on the subject. "There is great danger with illegals but I have a great relationship with Hispanics and Latinos. I'll take back all the jobs from China and Japan and the Hispanics will get those jobs." It was an off-script and a risky statement, given the anti-immigrant feelings of Trump's seemingly core supporters. But never let it be said that Trump could not surprise if he felt a change-up would work better than a fastball.

With his sense of the exaggerated and dramatic, he also used the occasion to focus on how brave he could be, fighting the good fight in the backyard of the perceived enemy. "I'm putting myself in great danger by being here," he told reporters. "But I have to do it."

The visit to Nuevo Laredo was supposed to include a guided tour and conversation with border patrol agents who worked the area Trump was visiting.

To Trump's way of thinking, it most likely would have made a great photo op. But when the union representing the border patrol agents canceled the agent's participation, Trump, as noted in the Associated Press, was quick to turn on them when he said, "The union canceled because they were afraid, because they were afraid to say what was really going on at the border."

After a quick, heavily police escorted motorcade tour around the area, Trump was whisked back to his private plane and was once again in the air and onto his next meeting with the masses. To Trump's way of thinking, his one-hour stopover in Nuevo Laredo had been a success, because he felt he had made his point.

Chapter Eighteen
Donald Loves Megyn?

Trump has never suffered fools or full-frontal attacks lightly. An over-the-top putdown was usually all it took, at least to the media's way of thinking, to make the pesky annoyance to Trump's ego go away. But late in July, *The Des Moines Register* struck a bit too close to home for Trump when they ran an editorial suggesting in no uncertain terms that Trump was a joke and an embarrassment and that he should get out of the race.

Trump's response? Freedom of the press be damned.

The Trump team had *The Des Moines Register's* press credentials for an upcoming campaign stop pulled and strongly intimated that the paper might get their privileges back if they followed Trump's rules. Trump, in a Des Moines Register report, called the paper's coverage of him "uneven," "inconsistent" and "dishonest." "I am not at all surprised by *The Des Moines Register's* sophomoric editorial. They will do anything for a headline and this paper's "non-endorsement" got them some desperately needed ink."

To what degree Trump's slap on the wrist has affected the paper's coverage of Trump is uncertain. But the reality is that, over the years, Trump's outgoing nature has curried a lot of favor with media types, especially those with the propensity for being to the right of center, especially Fox News. Trump has been a regular on several Fox News shows and, along the way, became the go to guest when they needed 'an authority' to validate the station's point of view. Which is why, when it was announced that the first Republican debate would be sponsored by Fox News and paneled by several of Fox News' program hosts, Trump must have figured that he was in for a fairly stress-free ride.

At least that's what he thought. But he must have underestimated Megyn Kelly.

Megyn was considered a rising star on the television news stage. She was bright, intelligent, took her job seriously and did her homework. Unlike other hosts who had gained a reputation for agenda-driven reporting, Megyn gravitated toward doing her homework and making interview subjects squirm for the betterment and honesty of a story.

Trump and Megyn were not strangers.

"In the past, he would send me press clippings about me that he would just sign Donald Trump," she recalled in a recent *Vanity Fair* profile. "And he called me from time to time to compliment a segment. I didn't know why he was doing that. And then he announced that he was running for president, it became clearer. But I can't be wooed. I was never going to love him, and I was never going to hate him."

But as she prepped for the debate, she did have a plan of attack.

For the remainder of the Republican candidates, the August 6 debate was their first best chance to finally be heard on a national stage. They realized much of the media was Trump's bitch and they would have to fight tooth and nail to get their points across through the din of the expected Trump shenanigans. They also realized that even if a question were directed at them, Trump would be waiting in the wings to respond and steal their thunder.

Not long after the debate started, Trump was already stirring the pot. When moderator Bret Baier asked all those candidates to raise their hand if they would promise to support the Republican nominee and not run as a third party candidate, the only one who did not raise their hand was Trump. Trump indicated that he would make that decision only after he determined how well he was treated by the Republican Party. His remarks were met by a scattering of boos and immediate accusatory responses from other candidates. Trump had suddenly become the center of attention, which was how he planned it all along.

Despite this outburst, Trump would remain largely subdued but no less responsive throughout most of the debate...

Until it was Megyn's turn to question Trump. Megyn had done her homework and had found he had a fairly long and detailed history of disparaging women, a list she read to Trump's face.

"You've called women you don't like fat pigs, dogs, slobs and disgusting animals. You once told a contestant on *Celebrity Apprentice* it would be a pretty picture to see her on her knees. Does that sound to you like the temperament of a man we should elect as President and how will you answer the charge of Hillary Clinton that you are part of the war on women?"

It looked as if Trump was surprised by the question, but laughed it off by saying that those descriptions were directed at comedian and television personality Rosie O'Donnell. But Megyn kept at him, which ruffled his feathers and brought what many within earshot considered an outright threat.

"Honestly Megyn, if you don't like it, I'm sorry. I've been very nice to you, although I could probably, maybe, not be based on the way you've treated me."

Trump may well have thought Megyn's attack would have a shelf life of about an hour. But when polls and Facebook and text messages immediately following the debate showed that women were now a bit shaky on Trump and his alleged anti-woman stance, Trump most likely sensed he was in the middle of a firestorm that would not soon go away. And so he continued to attack and, in the eyes of many, sink to a new low.

The next night Trump, in an interview with CNN, suggested that the reason Megyn had been so "hostile" to him was that she was probably menstruating. "You could see there was blood coming out of her eyes, blood coming out of her wherever." Megyn remained professional and above Trump's attacks, most likely sending Trump's ego into a tailspin. Trump was not finished. He began a texting and tweeting attack on the reporter, calling her "a lightweight" and "a bimbo." When that only succeeded in driving up Megyn's prestige and, by association, her ratings, Trump called on his followers to boycott her show.

What Trump might well have not planned on was that his followers might take matters into their own hands. Megyn was bombarded with death threats, cries of "cunt" and "hag." One of Trump's top deputies, Michael Cohen, was even caught tweeting the phrase "gut her."

By all accounts, Trump may well have won that first debate, but in the process he exposed the world to a very dark, petulant and ugly side.

Chapter Nineteen
Ups and Downs

Not that Trump seemed all that concerned, and the polls seemed to bear out the fact that, despite the Megyn Kelly flap, Trump had emerged from that first debate fairly unscathed.

Polls taken by NBC News and Reuters indicated that Trump was polling a solid 23% of Republican support while his two nearest opponents, Ben Carson and Ted Cruz, were a distant second and third. An even more encouraging poll in mid-August indicated that in the swing states (states recognized as being important in a national election) of Florida, Ohio and Pennsylvania, Trump was ahead of or barely trailing the Democratic favorite Hillary Clinton.

But an ABC News/*Washington Post* poll issued around the same time told a much different story. According to the figures, 64% of women voters looked at Trump unfavorably and 74% of non -white voters saw Trump in a negative light. Given what many considered his blatantly racist statements on immigration, coupled with his recent tiff with Megyn Kelly, it was not surprising that Trump was not doing well with those important voting blocks. But if Trump was sweating those negative stats, he didn't show it.

He had a fanatic following who showed up at every rally, cheered his every statement and proclamation and were quick on Twitter to protest any perceived attack against Trump. To many, it was as if Trump were operating in a parallel universe, a Teflon world in which he saw himself as immune from any negative attacks. Trump continued to be arrogant in the campaign and essentially uninterested in any perceived attack on his character. Which for Trump was fine, despite the fact that post debate, he continued to be in the eye of a storm of non-stop controversy.

The next stumble proved to be a profile on Trump *in Rolling Stone* in which it described a scene in which Trump is watching a news show when Carly Fiorina appeared on screen. Trump's response to the reporter sitting with him was, "Look at that face! Would anyone vote for that? Can you imagine that the face of our next President? I mean she's a woman and I'm not supposed to say bad things. But really folks! C'mon! Are you serious?"

The press jumped on the quote and it was not long before Fiorina responded on a Fox News program hosted by Megyn Kelly. "I think those comments speak for themselves. Maybe I'm getting under his skin a bit because I'm climbing in the polls."

Fiorina's comeback must have pricked Trump's normally thick skin because at a Hampton, New Hampshire rally (reported by BloombergPolitics.com) he responded in what appeared to be the same threatening tone he had used on Megyn during the debate. "Carly was a little nasty to me. Be careful Carly. Be careful."

The fallout of Trump's attack on Megyn would

have immediate repercussions. Initially scheduled to speak at a conference for an influential activist group, Red State, Trump was suddenly disinvited by the organization's founder Erick Erickson. Trump dismissed Erickson as "a total loser."

The Trump slide continued when, as reported by CNN and other outlets, Trump's senior counsel Michael Cohen, responding to an article in The Daily Beast alleging Trump may have raped his first wife, stated, "You cannot rape your spouse." The uproar was immediate and widespread. Cohen immediately backtracked, apologizing for the comment. Trump, in a CNN interview, stated flatly, "Michael Cohen does not speak for me." But it was too late and Trump, in the eyes of many, was now in the crosshairs of one of the groups he most wanted in his corner.

By this time, it had turned into open season on anything Trump and anti-women, and CNN did their due diligence in digging up a story from 2011 in which Trump reportedly lambasted a female lawyer during a deposition for wanting to take a break so she could pump breast milk for her child. According to the report, Trump told the lawyer, "You're disgusting."

Trump's campaign infrastructure took a big hit in August when long-time Trump advisor Roger Stone was let go by the campaign on the grounds that he was using the campaign to draw publicity to himself and away from the goals of the campaign. But if Trump's campaign was suddenly in seeming disarray, you could not tell it from his popular support. In mid-September, Trump would hold a massive outdoor rally in Alabama that drew an estimated 30,000 people, some from as far away as Los Angeles. As reported by

CNN and other outlets, the rally was typical Trump, attacking his opponents, undocumented immigrants, terrorism, jobs, the military and taking a few shots at the media along the way. Trump did not deviate from his tried and true stream of consciousness pitch. And there was no reason that he should, because he had packed the house with true believers who were there with Trump at every turn.

Love him or hate him, Trump knew how to get an audience into the figurative palm of his hand. The question remained, could he get them to the voting booth?

Consequently, there was a real sense of urgency when the candidates lined up at the Ronald Reagan Library on September 15 for the second debate. Many of the candidates knew that they could no longer stand back and deal with Trump's barbs and not fight back. Whether or not Trump felt he could skate through another debate on the strength of his entertainment and celebrity value is not certain. But what was immediately evident as the debate began was that Trump was going to give as good as he got. Jeb Bush, who had been sinking in the polls largely due to a perceived lack of energy and excitement, would land some telling blows during a give and take with Trump on Trump's illegal immigration stance. Rand Paul also played out a verbally bloody exchange with Trump regarding how the government should be run.

Trump was at his best when he could trot out his expected shoot-from-the-hip comments and allegations and he was quick to say what he would do if elected President. However, keen observers of this verbal throw down were quick to point out that Trump was still maddeningly light on specifics of issues and the nuts and bolts and would fade into the background when the questions centered on specifics. It was clear that when forced to deal with how he would go about fixing things and could not coast on personality and what many considered his trademark bullying tactics, he had not done his homework.

Following the conclusion of the three-hour marathon debate, Trump was uncharacteristically complimentary to the other candidates and said he had enjoyed himself. But the reality was that Trump had suffered some significant blows to his campaign during the months of August and September and his showing that night had not been his finest hour. But as his private plane taxied off into the Southern California skies, Trump had to feel comforted by two facts. He was still ahead in the polls and he was off to the heartland where he had the crowds, the enthusiasm and the die-hard followers.

Those were people who flocked to his rhetoric and bombast, his true strengths, and would, most certainly, support him to the end.

Chapter Twenty
Trump's Scapegoat

Into late August and early September, things seemed to be getting a bit tense in Trump's world. Not that Trump would acknowledge such a blasphemy. Everything was fine. He was doing well in the polls and he was going to win. That was his ongoing mantra, staccato pronouncements that could not be shaken. But the reality and/or perception was that the Trump show was getting a bit tired.

He was still comfortably ahead in most polls, but the margins seemed to be ever so slightly shrinking. Even as some of the lesser Republican candidates were dropping out of the race or who were teetering in single digits, a handful of competitors, notably Ted Cruz and Marco Rubio, had begun to present themselves as viable alternatives. And it was something that Trump could not help but think about.

Trump had eventually caved in to the Republican parties' loyalty pledge, that would indicate his support for whoever the Republican candidate might be as well as hold him to a promise not to run as an independent He signed on the dotted line, but even as he did so, he indicated that an independent run was not out of the question if he felt he had not been treated fairly by the Republicans. Reading between the lines, there was a sense of defiance and maybe fear in the notion that the Republicans might, somehow, turn on him and that by jumping to an independent run, which many have predicted would cost the Republicans the election, he would get even.

In an attempt, perhaps, to soften his often prickly image, Trump trotted out his wife and kids for some softball interviews during the month of September and into October, in which his family was effusive in what a wonderful husband and father he was and what a great president he would be. But all the warm and fuzzy moments in the world could not take away from the fact that Trump's run for The White House was still a contact sport.

As the months ticked down to the start of primary season, protestors against just about everything that came out of Trump's mouth became more plentiful and more aggressive. Which ultimately led to a couple of physical confrontations between protestors (and journalists) as reported by the likes of CNN,CNBC and *The Washington Post*. On August 21, Trump's chief of security, Keith Schiller forcibly ejected Univision journalist Jorge Ramos, reportedly at Trump's order, when the candidate objected to Ramos' line of questioning. September 3 would bring more security toughness when Schiller was filmed punching a protestor outside of Trump Tower. Of the latter incident, Trump's spokespeople reported that Schiller had been acting in self-defense after the protestor had chased after Schiller and jumped on his back. Like everything else in Trump's world, it only took a couple of news cycles for the rough stuff to be replaced in the public's mind by something else; immigration and terrorism.

Trump continued to flog both at every speaking opportunity. It had become evident to seasoned media observers that Trump's campaign to this point had been playing, primarily, to an audience of blue collar workers, many on the lower economic scale, who were essentially anti-government and, very often, rabid in their dislike of foreigners. But verbally beating on Mexicans and terrorism was beginning to sound old and a bit tired to those who wanted a little meat (i.e. solutions) to go along with their rhetoric and flag waving.

Trump needed something to jumpstart his campaign and keep him in the headlines. Fortunately for Trump, world events would step in with the terrorist attacks in Paris and, some weeks later, the attack in San Bernardino, California, that left 14 dead and many wounded at the hands of two radicalized Muslims. Trump saw an opening and quickly made his feelings on the matter public.

In early December, mere days after the San Bernardino attack, Trump said that if it were up to him, all Muslims would be banned from entering the United States. As reported by Reuters, CNN and countless other national and international media outlets, Trump stated, "I call for a complete shutdown of Muslims entering the country until our countries' representatives can figure out what is going on. Until we are able to determine and understand this problem and the dangerous threats it poses, our country cannot be the victim of horrendous attacks by people who have no respect for human life."

Reuters sent an email to Trump's campaign manager Corey Lewandowski asking for clarification if Trump's ban would include all immigration, student visas, tourists and all manner of other travelers. It elicited a one word response. "Everyone."

Trump's comments had the desired effect. It reignited the whole terrorism and immigration issue among a large percentage of Republican voters (as well as many non-Republicans), as the media put his comments in big headlines all over the world and, as if Trump needed more exposure at this point, made him an instant must-have interview in the press where he would reiterate his feeling about banning Muslims.

Trump, in an interview with *Good Morning America*, cited President Franklin D. Roosevelt's use of the Alien and Sedition Acts following the attack on Pearl Harbor in 1941. Roosevelt issued Executive Orders 2525, 2526 and 2527, according to which noncitizens of Japanese, German and Italian descent were detains and Executive Order 9066, which led to the internment of Japanese-Americans. "What I'm doing is no more different than what FDR did in his day," said Trump. "I don't like doing it at all. It would be a temporary measure until our representatives, many of whom are grossly incompetent, can figure out what's going on."

Trump's proposed Muslim ban brought the ire of many and, yes, some measure of guarded support, from fellow presidential candidates and world leaders alike. Many world leaders would evoke a fascist comparison and images of Japanese internment camps in rebuking Trump in countless news articles, including *People* and MSNBC

House Speaker Paul Ryan said in a press conference, "Trump's plan violates the constitution and is not who we are as a party." Hillary Clinton tweeted that Trump's idea was "reprehensible," "prejudiced" and "divisive." Senator Lindsey Graham, another candidate for the Republican nomination, told an MSNBC reporter, "Trump's actions are very inappropriate. You need to look the guy in the eye and say 'Listen, I don't agree with you.'"Speaking at a conference, Carly Fiorina stated, "It's a violation of our constitution. But it also undermines the character of our nation. Republican National Committee Chairman Reince Priebus, who most likely had already lost a lot of sleep since Trump entered the race, told The Washington Examiner, "We need to take on radical Islamic terrorism but not at the expense of our American values."

Even countries such as Canada, France and England, who normally make a point of not commenting on the particulars of US politics, joined the chorus condemning Trump's anti-Muslim stance. UK Labor Leader Jeremy Corbyn was particularly agitated when he tweeted, "Mr. Trump's call was an attack on Democratic values and an affront to common humanity."

The United Kingdom took their anger at Trump a decidedly serious step further when a country-wide petition was circulated that asked for Trump to never be allowed to enter the UK again. By law, a minimum of 100,000 signatures was needed for the topic to be debated in Parliament. More than 500,000 signatures were collected. A three-hour debate was held and the notoriously staid Parliament members were taken to such outbursts as calling Trump "crazy" and "offensive." Ultimately it would be a futile exercise that ended without a vote because Parliament, by law, was not allowed to enact such a ban.

Well into December, Trump was picking up as many supporters and as detractors, among them one of the more notorious contestants from his *The Apprentice* years, Omarosa Manigault. The mouthy and successful alumni was at Trump's side in mid-month when Trump gathered more than one hundred African American ministers at a meeting in New York City. In a later interview on *The Steve Harvey Show*, Omarosa declared her support for Trump when she said, "In terms of him running for president, it's something he always wanted to do, it's a dream. I want to help him achieve that dream. I'm a very loyal person."

Meanwhile, as far as Trump was concerned, the whole world could rail at him and call him names. Because Trump, according to an ABC/*Washington Post* poll taken shortly after the controversy started, indicated that not only did 59% of Republican voters support Trump's anti-Muslim views but 36% of the country as a whole was on Trump's side.

For Trump it was shaping up as a very Merry Christmas.

Chapter Twenty-One
Trump Takes Aim

Into the New Year, things were getting tight.

It was to be expected that some Republican candidates would drop out, and they did. What had started out as a very long laundry list was now a very manageable two-digit list. But that did not stop things from getting tense and contentious as the remaining candidates crisscrossed the country. With the initial state primaries in Iowa and New Hampshire now only weeks away, many of the frontrunners began spending an increasing amount of time in those two states. The speeches, for the most part, were now quite familiar, with familiar promises, pledges and solutions being thrown out in hopes of snagging the undecided voter.

And depending on the latest poll results, Trump was more than willing to get down in the dirt. While still seemingly holding comfortable leads over his Republican rivals, the numbers seemed to be ever so slightly shrinking. For a time, Ben Carson's numbers were rising and he seemed a legitimate threat to Trump. And that's when Trump began reverting from a stance of being friends with his fellow candidates to slamming and slamming hard.

Speaking to a group in the later part of 2015, Trump hinted at Carson's Seventh Day Adventist religion as something that potential voters should be concerned about adding no small sense of innuendo to his speech covered by *The New York Times*. "I don't know about Seventh Day Adventists," Trump said in an almost conspiratorial tone. "I just don't know." Whether this speech had anything to do with Carson's sudden and fairly rapid decline in the polls is not certain. But casting that kind of doubt certainly did not help.

These kinds of hit and run attacks are nothing new for Trump. His history has shown that whenever faced with an uncomfortable situation or a question he can't answer. His dealings with Rosie O' Donnell are a prime example as were the most recent issue with Megyn Kelly. In Trump's world it is often attack and attack again.

And as it would turn out, such attacks were not exclusive to his own party. Shortly after Hillary Clinton announced that her husband, former President Bill Clinton, would be on the campaign trail, campaigning for her in pivotal states, Trump began attacking the former President's series of alleged affairs throughout the years. And as reported by the likes of *Face the Nation* and ABC News, said attacks were vicious.

In one diatribe, Trump accused Bill Clinton of "being one of the great abusers of the world" and compared him to recently called out alleged sex abuser Bill Cosby. And in a tweet Trump raged, "If Hillary thinks she can unleash her husband with his terrible record with women abuse, while playing the women's card on me, she's wrong."

Trump was not finished with Clinton. During a speech in Michigan in early 2016, Trump raised the attack level by using the vulgar Yiddish word for a man's penis, schlonged, to describe how Obama beat Clinton in the 2008 campaign. Later in the diatribe, he also brought up the fact that, in the recent Democratic debate, Clinton was late getting back on stage after a commercial break, intimating that she was late getting back from a bathroom break. "I know where she went," he said as reported by CNN. "It's disgusting. I don't want to talk about it."

But, this night, Trump was not getting off free. Despite playing to an audience of primarily hardcore Trump followers, a number of anti-Trump protestors had managed to get into the hall and would, periodically, interrupt Trump with boos and anti-Trump statements. Trump responded to the catcalls by calling them "a bunch of losers."

But easily the most ambitious Trump attacks were directed at Republican competitor Ted Cruz. The Texas Senator was proving to be a tough competitor who had, largely, avoided Trump's attacks by keeping a relatively low but consistent profile while waging a campaign based on the issues. The result was that by the beginning of 2016, Cruz had pulled to within four points of Trump in Iowa polls, a statistical tie. Cruz was good in dealing with evangelical voters in the state; Trump seemed to be learning on the job and his lack of Trump-like bombast was, to many, ultimately a more logical choice in the upcoming primaries.

Trump would never say that he was concerned. In fact, the media had noted that Cruz and Trump had had a cordial friendship during the early stages of the campaign. But it soon became obvious that he was most certainly aware of Cruz's strengths. Which is why, shortly after the New Year, the attacks on Cruz began. "The truth is that Ted Cruz is a nasty guy," said Trump as reported by *The New York Times*. "Nobody likes him. Nobody in Congress likes him. He has an edge that is not good. It's not a good thing for the country."

Trump would continue the verbal assault, citing a 2012 loan from the firm Goldman Sachs, which employed Cruz's wife at the time, of a million dollars to help finance his Senate campaign that same year, but which he failed to report in Federal Election Commission documents. And, in a thinly veiled repeat of his 'birther' comments against Obama some years earlier, he openly questioned whether Cruz was eligible to run for President because, he had been born in Canada to an American mother.

Much like Clinton had done, Cruz took the high road, admonishing Trump for his unwarranted charges. Trump's attacks, to many observers, were not showing him in his most presidential light. But he seemed like a dog with a bone, continuing to publically speak out about Cruz at campaign stops. But more and more people seemed to tire of what many perceived as Trump's mouth and the circus-like atmosphere that seemed to follow him everywhere he went.

In the wake of Trump's anti-Muslim sentiment Rose Hamid, a Muslim woman, dressed in a white and teal headscarf, went to a Trump speech and stood up in the midst of an ugly crowd and stood silently so, she would say later, that people could see what a real Muslim looked like. As she was escorted out by security amid the screams and taunts of the crowd, Trump stood smiling.

Trump and Cruz, as scheduling would have it,

both appeared at a Tea Party Convention. Two hours after Cruz spoke, Trump took the stage and, almost immediately, began attacking Cruz. The response was boos cascading down on Trump.

Trump seemed momentary taken aback. But just as quickly he was back on autopilot, talking the standard Trump line as if nothing had happened.

The final two weeks before the Iowa primary kicked off, Trump's stretch run to a possible nomination was turning particularly ugly. At that point Trump and Cruz were considered the co-frontrunners with Rubio lurking slightly on the outside looking in. But it was primarily Trump and Cruz who were going at it, hammer and tongs with non-stop television ads and a whole lot of nasty verbal attacks. And the Republican Party as a whole was choosing up sides.

More and more the consensus was that Trump was suddenly a legitimate candidate worthy of both respect and fear. The scenario was dubious in either case. To suddenly throw all their weight behind a Trump candidacy was repugnant to many of the old guard in the GOP. But to slam Trump at this point could easily spell disaster as a whole, with Trump going rogue or independent, whichever way you want to look at it.

The August publication of the right-leaning *National Review* took a courageous step when it came out with an entire issue, consisting of 22 essays by noted practitioners of editorial and political notoriety, each directing their best reasons why Trump should not be the Republican nominee. In typical Trump fashion, he dismissed the magazine and the contributors in a *New York Times* quote as "a failing publication and a bunch of losers."

Trump's response was equally outrageous and no less brave when he brought Sarah Palin on stage during a speech to officially pledge her support for Trump's candidacy. For many the brash and outrageous Palin, who many remember for her lack of political acumen when she was running for vice president alongside John McCain, was the female equivalent of Trump. It seemed like a match made in heaven or hell.

Just when things in Trump's world could not seem to get any more surreal, up popped another billionaire, former New York mayor Michael Bloomberg who, in an Associated Press story, was suddenly making noises about getting into the race as an independent because of his growing concern that the candidates in both the Republican and Democratic camps (particularly Trump and Bernie Sanders) might negatively impact the country and, particularly, Wall Street. Observers of the political scene were suddenly salivating at the possibility of two billionaires duking it out as independents in the midst of already chaotic Republican and Democratic races.

But Trump did not seem perturbed by the sudden increase in political craziness as the clocks wound down to the polls opening in Iowa. In fact, in one of his final Iowa appearances, Trump made it clear that he was the frontrunner and that nobody was going to take that away from him.

"I could stand in the middle of Fifth Avenue and shoot somebody and I wouldn't lose any voters," Trump told the crowd, reported in an Associated Press story. There were few in the crowd that would argue his point.

Chapter Twenty-Two
The Final Countdown

The Iowa primary was less than two weeks away. Although he was beginning to spend more and more time in Nevada and South Carolina, part of the next wave of state primaries, he was seemingly racking up frequent flyer miles between Iowa and New Hampshire, stumping for every vote he could get. There was excitement in the air, and a whole lot of speculation.

The consensus among seasoned political observers was that Iowa was too close to call between the two frontrunners, Trump and Cruz. New Hampshire, always a wild card in political years, seemed to be wavering between Trump, Cruz and Rubio, who had made great strides below the radar. But ultimately talk and conjecture usually began and ended with Trump.

Those inclined to look into the future speculated that Trump victories in Iowa and New Hampshire would signal that the mogul would most certainly run the table on the rest of the states and be the unanimous choice for Republican nominee for President. Many were looking at that possibility with dread; speculating that Trump had already caused so much infighting and damage to a Republican Party that was already perceived as old and out of touch with the real world, that the GOP might well lose control of both houses of Congress in upcoming elections, whether or not Trump made it to the White House.

Then there is that little matter of Trump running as a third party candidate. Trump had long maintained that, despite signing the Republican Party's loyalty pledge, he was not necessarily tied to the notion of helping the person that might beat him out and that he would bolt if he felt he had not been treated fairly. Losing the nomination would seem to translate Trump being treated unfairly and Trump going out as a third party independent would almost guarantee a Republican loss at the polls.

The 'silly season' of Republican politics was manifesting itself in several offbeat bits of pop culture merchandizing and novelty items. Easily the most notorious and largely successful of these had to be a gay-themed erotic novel going under the title *Trump Temptations: The Billionaire And The Bellboy*. Written by 22-year-old Los Angeles comedian Elijah Daniel who, according to reports in *The Los Angeles Times* and *The Guardian*, concocted a hilarious tale of gay seduction between the real estate magnate and a bellboy in Hong Kong in a four-hour writing jag fueled by lots of alcohol. The joke has been wildly successful as the book currently sits high atop Amazon rankings in the categories of humorous erotica and gay erotic.

Trump was too busy to deal with what he considered idle speculation. He was too busy trying to cover all his bases. A big announcement of support had come three weeks into the New Year when controversial former vice presidential candidate Sarah Palin threw her support behind Trump. Once people stopped laughing at Palin's outrageous rants, they realized that there just might not be a lot to laugh at. Trump would also make an appearance at the evangelical Christian Liberty University, founded by Jerry Falwell, where he would be largely restrained rather than outlandish, hoisting the Bible as he proclaimed his religious background and how the bible guided him in his daily life.

It seemed ironic that the last days before the first state primary, Trump was casting his lot with God. The world was waiting for God's reply.

Chapter Twenty-Three
Today Iowa, Tomorrow the World

Trump seemed pretty sure of himself going into the Iowa caucuses. The latest polls had given him a commanding lead and he was continuing to draw large crowds. And so he figured he could go ahead and skip the final Republican debate, just days before Iowans would caucus for the all- important delegate votes.

Trump's decision to pass on the debate, sponsored by Fox News, began when it was announced that Megyn Kelly would be the moderator. Trump carried a grudge and, truth be known, the aftermath of their initial debate blow-up had hurt him with women and exposed a side of him that he, most certainly, did not want aired. Trump wavered for a few days about whether he would show or not and hinted that he might do a counter rally to the Fox debate to raise money for veterans' groups. But when Fox News honcho Roger Ailes released a tweet taking shots at, among other things, Trump's ability to be President, the school yard brawl reached critical mass and Trump, officially, pulled out of the debate.

Which, ultimately, proved a plus for the rest of the candidates. With the "800 pound gorilla" now out of the room, the debate among the other candidates proved a spirited give and take in which actual issues were discussed and candidates, in a positive, enlightening way, agreed to disagree.

Trump's "counter programming," would reportedly raise an estimated $6 million for the veterans and cast Trump in a positive charitable light that, when coupled with his recent overtures to Iowa's evangelical religious community, seemed to put him in good stead for the February 1st caucus.

But from the moment they began counting ballots, it was apparent that the will of the people had turned in another direction. After leading momentarily with the early ballots cast, Trump quickly dropped to second place behind a resurgent Cruz and was struggling throughout the night to, both, catch up and to keep ahead of Rubio who, from the beginning, was nipping at Trump's heels.

The reality was that by the end of the first hour of ballot reports, Trump had sunk to four points behind Cruz and would finally manage to hang on to second by a mere point by the night's end. Journalists and political pundits began to smell blood in the water and were quick to dissect why the favorite candidate had not captured Iowa.

Many attributed Trump's MIA at the recent debate as a reason voters were having second thoughts about Trump and his character and sincerity. Others speculated that it was Trump's insistence on large gatherings and spectacle rather than the more traditional, "boots on the ground" get the vote out, a tactic effectively employed by Cruz, Rubio and others. Whatever the reason, Trump was almost immediately cast in a vulnerable light and, consequently, would be an ever-increasing target from other candidates and, perhaps supporters, who may have suddenly felt that Trump's approach to politics was getting stale.

Trump conceded the night in an unusually non-Trump like concession speech later in the evening, downright humble in the face of his first real setback but promising with only mild bluster that he would still win the nomination and beat anybody who the Democrats put up against him.

Trump made his way to his private plane and headed off to the next stop on the campaign trail, the New Hampshire caucuses scheduled for February 9th. Trump was favored in New Hampshire by a fairly substantial margin. But New Hampshire was notorious for its independent nature and, as Iowa had proven that in politics nothing was certain.

Chapter Twenty-Four
Snow-blind in Dixville Notch

Dixville Notch, New Hampshire is an unincorporated community as far up as you can go, some 20 miles as the crow flies, from the Canadian border. The population, as of 2010, was 12. Outside of its unusual name, Dixville Notch, to most is little more than an obscure blip on the map.

But every four years, Dixville Notch morphs into something special and important, the first town to cast the first ballots for candidates in New Hampshire. And so, shortly after midnight and into February 9th, the entire voting population of Dixville Notch gathered in a very tiny meeting room and cast their ballots.

A total of five ballots were cast for Republicans. Three votes went to Kasich. Two votes went to Trump.

Not that the first vote meant a lot despite a long standing urban legend that the winner of the Dixville Notch ballot inevitably made his or her way to The White House. But it made for a good story and the occasion of the Dixville Notch vote signaled the start of a primary vote whose state was rife with unpredictability. New Hampshire voters for historically notorious for their contrary and unpredictable nature when it came time to vote. Only slightly surprising was the fact that more New Hampshire voters had declared themselves either Independent or Undecided than all declared Republican and Democratic voters combined. And the former were stubbornly refusing to lean one way or the other until the moment they stepped into the voting booth. And, as far as Trump and his advisors were concerned, this year would be no different.

Despite the shock of Trump finishing second in Iowa. Trump, according to recent polls, still held a healthy, double digit lead going into New Hampshire. But, to many observers, it was still shaping up as too close to call. Cruz and Rubio were seemingly head to head for second and third place finishes while the likes of Bush, Kasich, Christie and others, sensing that a New Hampshire loss could be their Waterloo, were turning the normally sedate fields of New Hampshire into a political death match, hurtling insults, innuendo and the occasional political facts of life at each other like so many grenades.

But the reality was that the polls opened, New Hampshire was in the midst of a driving winter punctuated by curtains of equally blistering snowstorms. New Hampshire and bad weather was nothing new. How said weather would impact voter turnout was a whole other matter.

For his part, Trump did not seem to be worried. A mixture of trademark arrogance sprinkled an amazingly softer and accommodating side peppered the state with appearances, playing his trademark defiance to much smaller halls and diners and working real hard to convince people that he was just like them. There were the last minute appearances into the early afternoon before Trump retired to await the results.

And it would not be long before he discovered that he had struck the right chord in the Granite State. Within an hour of the polls closing, early tallies indicated that Trump had built up a sizeable lead that he would not relinquish throughout the night. His closest competitor, John Kasich, was a distant second while Cruz, Bush and the suddenly nose-diving Rubio spent the evening vying for a closely contested third. But none of that was of concern to Trump. From the outset, New Hampshire had been his and all the media speculation about what might happen if he somehow lost or was not far and away the winner could not change the fact that Trump was now in the win column.

Trump's victory lap was an alternately heartfelt and vintage Trump speech in front of New Hampshire loyalists. He trotted out his usual tropes of illegal immigration, pro-life, bringing back jobs and building the wall across the US/Mexican border. But he was also humble this next time, thanking his entire family, important team members and the voters who had supported him and made the night the first of what he predicted would be the first of many victories on the road to The White House.

"Now it's on to South Carolina," he closed. "Thank you very much. I love you. I love you all."

Chapter Twenty-Five
Trump Takes the South

By the time Trump's private jet touched down in South Carolina, things were beginning to get real ugly in Trump's always-unpredictable world.

Audiences for Trump's rallies were less accommodating and his remarks were often greeted by boos. Trump lashed out at the Republican Party higher ups, suggesting that they had papered his audiences with Republican donors who were anti Trump. He immediately took his perccived slight personally and, in yet another turn of temperament, suggested once again that he might decide to run as an Independent if the party did not bow down to him. Trump's anger was further fueled by media observers who were falling in line behind the notion that no Republican candidate would reach the magic number of delegates and that the ultimate candidate might be brokered at convention time in a much dreaded option, 'the back room deal.'

The tone of South Carolina had become extremely vicious between Trump and his perceived closest competitors, Cruz and Rubio, with insults between the trio now increasingly nasty and personal. And in one particularly heated exchange, Trump, indirectly, went one-on-one with the Pope.

While on a goodwill tour of Mexico, Pope Francis was asked what he thought about Trump putting up a wall to keep illegal immigrants out of the US. In an Associated Press article, Pope Francis responded, "A person who thinks only about building walls, wherever they may be, and not building bridges, is not a real Christian."

During a stop in South Carolina, Trump immediately responded by saying "For a religious leader to question a person's faith is disgraceful." He further acknowledged in his Associated Press response that the prospect of ISIS possibly attacking The Vatican might cause Pope Francis to change his attitude. "If that happened, the Pope would have only wished and prayed that Donald Trump would have been president because this would not have happened."

In the days leading up to the South Carolina primary, Trump held a sizeable two-digit lead over his rivals and the pundits were suddenly in lockstep with the notion that a South Carolina victory would open the floodgates to a clean sweep of the upcoming primaries and an unabated march to the Republican nomination for president.

The pundits, to a very large extent, would be proven correct.

From the moment the South Carolina polls closed, Trump had moved to the front of the rapidly dwindling Republican pack and within an hour, the Associated Press, followed shortly by CNN, had declared Trump the winner with less than four percent of the votes counted, leaving the only lingering interest of the night the hotly contested battle for second place between Rubio and Cruz with Rubio winning out by two tenths of a percentage point.

Trump was joyous in a victory that would also be considered, for better or worse, a turning point for the Republican Party. He had arrived as the ultimate 'Teflon candidate' who could say anything but still be the darling of the masses. Trump told his followers in South Carolina that it was "a victory for the movement and a victory for the people." But he was quick to point out that there were many more battles to come, primarily the all- important march through the South that would take place in a matter of weeks. Battles he was confident he would win.

"Let's put this thing away!"

Epilogue
It's All Up To You

So there you have it. Donald Trump from before the cradle, to the cradle, and beyond as he stands on the precipice of political and historical greatness.

Or not.

If you did not get hip to the life and times of Donald Trump before discovering *The Apprentice*, the odds are good that you learned a lot. If you knew Trump way back in the day, the chances are good that you now know a whole lot more. But have you ultimately learned enough to walk into a voting booth and mark your X next to his name?

Maybe you have. Maybe you haven't. Maybe you already have and are now waiting along with everybody else on the planet for the final vote count. If you haven't, perhaps you're sitting alone in thought as you contemplate helping Donald Trump make history.

In the end…It's all up to you.

AFTERWARD
THE MOUTH THAT ROARED

Donald Trump has never met a person, place or thing he could not find something derogatory, nasty or unpleasant to say something about. *The New York Times*, in the name of good journalism, recently collected a who's who of Trump's targets and what he had to say about them. I leave you with some of Trump's subtle as a train wreck examples.

And you can always follow him on your own at @RealDonaldTrump on Twitter.

JEB BUSH
"He will do anything to stay at the trough.'
"He's a low energy guy."
"He should go home and relax."

BEN CARSON
"He is incapable of understanding foreign policy and very weak on illegal immigration."
"He has never created a job in his life."

HILLARY CLINTON
"She doesn't have the strength or stamina to be president."
"Her record is so bad."

181

TED CRUZ
"People do not like Ted."
"Goldman Sachs owns him."
"He would speak behind my back, get caught and then deny it."

CARLY FIORINA
"If you listen to Carly Fiorina for more than ten minutes you get a massive headache."

JOHN KASICH
"He's a dummy."
"He's one of the worst presidential candidates in history."

MARCO RUBIO
"He's a lightweight, a choker."
"He couldn't even respond properly to President Obama's State of The Union speech without pouring sweat and chugging water."

BERNIE SANDERS
"A wacko."

ARIANNA HUFFINGTON
"A liberal clown."

MEGYN KELLY
"She's a lightweight reporter."
"I refuse to call Megyn Kelly a bimbo because that would not be politically correct."

JOHN MCCAIN
"He's doing a lousy job of taking care of our vets."

RONDA ROUSEY
"Not a nice person."

SOURCES

BOOKS

The Art of The Deal by Donald J. Trump and Tony Schwartz (Random House 1987), *Never Enough*: *Donald Trump and The Pursuit of Success* by Michael D'Antonio (ThomasDunne 2015) ,*My New Order* by Adolph Hitler (Reynal and Hitchcock 1941*)*, *Mien Kamph* by Adolph Hitler (Reynal and Hitchcock 1929) *Trump: The Saga of America's Most Powerful Real Estate Baron* by Jerome Tuccille(Dutton 1985*)*, *The Trumps: Three Generations That Built An Empire* by Gwenda Blair (Simon & Schuster 2000*)*, *Donald Trump: Master Apprentice* by Gwenda Blair (Simon & Schuster 2005*)*, *Trump Nation: The Art of Being Donald* by Timothy O'Brien (Business Plus 2005), *The Art of The Comeback* by Donald Trump and Kate Bohner *(*Times Books 1997*)*, *Destiny and Power: The American Odyssey of George Herbert Walker Bush* by John Meacham (Random House 2015), *Think Big and Kick Ass in Business and in Life* by Donald Trump and Bill Zanker (Harper Collins) 2007

MAGAZINES

Rolling Stone, Vanity Fair, Spy, Up Here, Playboy, Adweek, New York Magazine, The National Review,

Women's Wear Daily, Cornell University Preservation News, Time, Newsday, Forbes, Money, The Atlantic, The National Review, Esquire

NEWSPAPERS/WIRE SERVICES
The New York Times, The Daily Mail, The Seattle Times, The Washington Post, The Globe, The Boston Globe, The Daily News, The Cincinnati Enquirer, The Sun Sentinel, The Baltimore Sun, The Daily News, AZQuotes.com, The National Enquirer, The Orlando Sentinel, British Sunday Times, USA Today, Associated Press, The Palm Beach Post, The New Hampshire Union Leader, The Huffington Post, The Des Moines Register, The Las Vegas Sun,

TELEVISION
CBS News, WNYW TV, *20/20, The Oprah Winfrey Show, Nightline, ABC News, The View, Fox and Friends, The Tonight Show, Fox News, The Today Show, NBC News, 7News Boston, 60 Minutes, This Week, CNBC, Good Morning America, MSNBC*

RADIO
National Public Radio, *The Hugh Hewitt Show*, *The Howard Stern Show*

WEBSITES
CNN.com, Gronda Morin.com, The Daily Beast.com, Politico.com, GeneologyAbout.com, Hubpages.com, The Real Deal.com, Business Insider.com, Trump's Education: Presidential Candidates.com, Truthdig.com, Political Tickerblogs. CNN, The Smoking Gun.com, Evan Carmichael.com, NYUEDU.com, Casino

Connection.com, Shagtree.com, Who Dated Who?com, EOnline.com, Inspirational Quotes About Life.com, Contactmusic.com, NewStraitsTimes.com, About Relationships.com, Ballot Access News.com, All Poltics.com, YahooPolitics.com, Yahoonews.com, The Economist/Yougov.com, Antiwar.com, Blackbag.com, Sec.gov.com, BloombergPolitics.com, Politifact.com, DonaldTrumpQuotesIMDB.com, CNN, Mashable.com, Salon.com, Foreword.com,

MISCELLANEOUS
USA Today/ Gallup Poll, Public Policy Poll, Extra Mile Casting Agency, Gotham Government Relations and Communications, Public Policy Polling Survey, ABC News/Washington Post Poll,

About the Author

New York Times bestselling author Marc Shapiro has written more than 60 nonfiction celebrity biographies, more than two-dozen comic books, numerous short stories and poetry and three short form screenplays. He is also a veteran freelance entertainment journalist.

His young adult book *JK Rowling: The Wizard Behind Harry Potter* was on *The New York Times* bestseller list for four straight weeks. His fact-based book *Total Titanic* was on *The Los Angeles Times* bestseller list for four straight weeks. *Justin Bieber: The Fever* was on the nationwide Canadian bestseller list for several weeks.

Shapiro has written books on such personalities as Shonda Rhimes, George Harrison, Carlos Santana, Annette Funicello, Lorde, Lindsay Johan, EL James, Jamie Dornan, Dakota Johnson, Adele and countless others. He also co-authored the autobiography of mixed martial arts fighter Tito Ortiz, *This Is Gonna Hurt: The Life of a Mixed Martial Arts Champion.*

He is currently working on updating his biographies of Gillian Anderson and Lucy Lawless for Riverdale Avenue Books.

Other Riverdale Avenue Books Titles by Marc Shapiro

The Secret Life of EL James

The Real Steele: The Unauthorized Biography of Dakota Johnson

Inside Grey's Anatomy: The Unauthorized Biography of Jamie Dornan

Annette Funicello: America's Sweetheart

Game: The Resurrection of Tim Tebow

Legally Bieber: Justin Bieber at 18

Lindsay Lohan: Fully Loaded, From Disney to Disaster

Lorde: Your Heroine, How This Young Feminist Broke the Rules and Succeeded

We Love Jenni: An Unauthorized Biography

Who Is Katie Holmes? An Unauthorized Biography
Norman Reedus: True Tales of The Waking Dead's Zombie Hunter,
An Unauthorized Biography

Welcome to Shondaland: An Unauthorized Biography of ShondaRhimes

34418750R00115

Made in the USA
Middletown, DE
20 August 2016